Who's Going to Watch My Kids?

·······

*Working Mothers' Humorous and
Heartfelt Struggles to Find and Hold on
to the Elusive Perfect Nanny*

Who's Going to Watch My Kids?

. . . .

Working Mothers' Humorous and
Heartfelt Struggles to Find and Hold on
to the Elusive Perfect Nanny

RACHEL LEVY LESSER

TURNING
STONE
PRESS

First published in 2015 by Turning Stone Press,
an imprint of Red Wheel/Weiser, LLC
With offices at:
665 Third Street, Suite 400
San Francisco, CA 94107
www.redwheelweiser.com

ISBN: 978-1-61852-094-4

Cover design by Jim Warner
Cover image: Woman: jane_Lane / shutterstock

Printed in the United States of America
10 9 8 7 6 5 4 3 2 1

Table of Contents

*For my girlfriends. For their stories,
their trust, and most especially for their
friendship. Life just wouldn't be as
much fun without you.*

Prologue

I never thought about nannies. I always knew that I wanted to have children one day, and I also always knew that I wanted a career. I just never thought about who would watch those children while I was having that career.

I first learned about nannies while still single, childless, and working at a large magazine company in New York City. I loved my boss, Jennifer. She was well respected by just about everyone in the company. She knew how to play the political games amongst the way-too-prevalent old boys' club in the office, but most of all she challenged me in my own work and taught me so much. And she was fun. She also had two young children and made it look so easy. She had a nanny.

The first time I met her nanny Louise was when Louise brought Jennifer's four-year-old son and six-month-old daughter in to the office. Louise wheeled them down the hall in their bright red double stroller, and we all oohhed and aahhed over their adorableness. We hung out in Jennifer's office for a few minutes while her son played with the desk toys, and Jennifer cuddled with her baby daughter. Then it was time for our weekly status meeting. Jennifer handed the baby back to nanny Louise. Before I got my notes together, the kids were kissed and strolled out of the office down the hall and off to wherever they went. It seemed like a great arrangement.

I wanted to be Jennifer one day—a successful and happy working mom. A woman who had it all. And of course I would be her, right? I had a good education, solid job experience, and I worked very hard. I was also in a serious relationship with a great guy who I suspected I would marry one day, and together we would have adorable children. Just like Jennifer's children, my future kids would get strolled in to my office one day by a smiley and loving nanny. I'd kiss them and play with them for a few minutes and then go about my day at work without a worry. It looked so easy and awesome. Then I had kids.

⌒ 1 ⌒

Search and Interview

I did end up marrying that great guy. He and I left New York City together just a couple years after getting hitched to attend business school at the University of Michigan in Ann Arbor. The great guy, Neil (his name is Neil, but I do still sometimes refer to him as that great guy), had always planned on getting his MBA as it was the next logical step in his career as a management consultant. I figured that earning my MBA would only help to advance my career in magazine marketing. Plus, I thought having that graduate degree would help me one day as a working mom.

Those days as a working mom came sooner than I had ever imagined. While I was living and studying in Ann Arbor, my mother was diagnosed with a very rare form of cancer back in Philadelphia near where I grew up. The cancer was aggressive and her prognosis was not good. I knew her days were numbered, and I wanted to be near her for as long as I could. I also wanted her to get to know her first grandchild if at all possible, as it would most likely be the only one she would ever know.

So I became pregnant during my second and last year as an MBA student and walked up to the podium to receive my Masters of Business Administration wearing a cap and gown and sporting a very pregnant belly. Prior to that graduation, Neil was offered a job in the Philadelphia office of the management consulting company he had worked for in New York before business school. That made the transition to be near my mother and the rest of my family relatively easy.

Just a few months after graduation, I gave birth to our first child—a boy named Joey. And as I had imagined long ago while working for the magazine company in New York, he was in fact adorable. I was pleased to see that baby Joey had a nicely shaped head and ears, or so other adults who seemed to know what they were talking about told me. Apparently I was not such a cute baby but, luckily, as my mother used to say, I outgrew that funny looking baby phase rather quickly.

It wasn't until Joey started sleeping through the night that I could begin to imagine myself working again. I couldn't think about anything beyond pumping breast milk and swaddling techniques before that magical morning when I awoke to a quiet house at 6 a.m. I immediately thought that the baby monitor had broken. Or worse, that Joey had lost his lung capacity and ability to cry. But he was fine. He was sleeping through the night at only six weeks old. I was so pleased with him and with myself too. When you first have a baby, everyone, from any friend you've ever known to complete strangers at the grocery store, will stop to ask you, "Is he sleeping through the night yet?" So when he did, and at quite an early age, I was pleased to answer with a resounding "yes."

I was lucky on the sleep front with Joey. He was a good eater and therefore a good sleeper. He still is now as an eleven-year-old child. As an infant he got enough nutrients during the day to make it through the night. Then I could sleep through the night again, and my brain started to function so I could go back to work. I had to go back—to earn an income and to keep my sanity.

I had looked for jobs throughout my pregnancy. At first I looked remotely from Michigan, and then in person once I was living in suburban Philadelphia. I thought that being pregnant would make it very difficult to land an interview, much less a job. I was lucky again—very lucky. The whole being pregnant thing forced me to be completely up-front with potential employers. I told them when I was due and that ideally I could start work three months after I gave birth. I put it all out there, and I was pleasantly surprised with many of the responses I received. I ended up getting an offer from a small marketing and strategic branding company just ten minutes from our house. My magazine marketing experience and MBA fit nicely in the business. We negotiated my salary and work schedule (three full days a week) during my pregnancy and agreed on a start date soon after Joey was born.

It all sounded great, and the sleep thing helped too, but then it was time for me to find my nanny Louise. I wasn't really sure how or where to find her. My mother suggested I contact a young woman named Stacey. Stacey's mother and my mother were friends, and Stacey had moved back to the area where she had grown up just like I did.

"In fact," my mother eagerly explained to me, "Stacey lives right around the corner from you. I think you two will really hit it off. She works too, and she has a nanny. A really good one I hear."

Is that all it takes to strike up a new friendship with another mom? I wondered. You just had to live near each other, work, and have a common interest in nannies? It kind of reminded me of the first week of college when you became friends with everyone on your freshman hall only because you shared a bathroom with them and walked the very same route to classes.

I was nervous to make the first move and call Stacey, but I was kind of desperate. I knew nothing about nannies and didn't really know anyone my age in Philly. I hadn't seen Stacey since she left for college when I was a freshman in high school, and I wasn't sure we had ever had a real conversation.

The Newspaper Ad

Stacey was more than happy to help me as our first real conversation went well. She had a lot of advice to give me on the nanny front, and I was happy to take it. She did remember me as the shy little kid that her friends used to babysit when we were growing up, and I think she still thought of me that way. I kind of did too as I wrote down almost every word out of her mouth, still thinking of her as the older and wiser girl who had been around the block a time or two. Since I had last seen Stacey in the late 1980s, she had moved away to go to college in the Midwest, and then to California where she worked in retail for nearly a decade. A job opportunity in her family's business eventually drew Stacey back to the Philadelphia area. When I first became reacquainted with Stacey, she had a toddler son and a baby boy on the way.

"Maybe our baby boys will be friends?" Stacey mentioned during that first phone conversation. I took that statement as the utmost compliment. I mean Stacey the older cool girl wanted her kid to hang out with mine? I had it made. All of those years of ignoring each other as kids just melted away. Almost immediately after our longer-than-expected first phone call ended, Stacey forwarded me the advertisement that she had placed in the local paper where she had found her first nanny. The nanny still worked for her some three years later, and Stacey made a point to tell me what a great feat that was. I wasn't so impressed. That didn't seem so long to me. I had worked at the magazine company in New York for six years and would have been there a lot longer had we not moved to Michigan for graduate school.

I took Stacey's ad, changed the days, hours, and contact information, and placed it in the same paper in which Stacey had placed her ad. That was it.

Nanny needed in home for baby

Mon, Wed, Fri 8:30 a.m.–6:30 p.m.

Experience and references necessary

Non-smoker, speaks English

Need driver's license and own car

Contact Information:

The ad ran on a Thursday, and the phone started ringing early Thursday morning. I scrambled for a pen to take down the candidates' information. I had a plan to screen each one over the phone, but that process was not as easy as I had imagined. Some of the women (and they were all women) gave me very little information, and some gave me way too much. I did my best to narrow my list down to a handful of candidates that I wanted to meet in person.

Eileen sounded like a lovely woman over the phone. She had experience in raising her then-grown children, and had taken care of her young grandchildren as well. I arranged an in-person meeting. She came to our house one bright and crisp fall afternoon. I was pleased that the weather was turning cooler and that I could fit into my pre-pregnancy favorite pair of jeans as I sat in the living room across from Eileen with baby Joey in my lap.

I had a list of interview questions borrowed from my new friend and nanny-finding mentor, Stacey. I revised the questions a bit to my liking but really tried to stick to her basic outline. I sort of felt like Stacey was my boss in the nanny-finding department, and I definitely needed one. Eileen spoke a lot about her children and grandchildren, and I liked that. When I asked about her professional experience it seemed that she had floated around from job to job. Perhaps her passion was in childcare, and she had just never found a job before in that field?

Our conversation soon turned to her involvement in her church, and I liked that sense of community involvement and giving back. But when she told me that she developed a strong connection to the church after years of battling alcoholism, I became skeptical. I didn't want to jump to any conclusions, but when you are interviewing someone to watch your new baby for nine plus hours a day alone in your home, and you find out that the person has pretty recently battled a heavy drinking problem, it's kind of a red flag. I couldn't help but stare at our small bar cart filled with bottles of alcohol that Eileen was sitting right next to as I held Joey now slightly closer to me. I imagined her taking a few swigs from the vodka bottle as she watched Joey, then swiftly refilling it with water like I once did in college when I was home visiting my parents.

I was all for giving someone a second chance, but not when my son's wellbeing could be at risk.

"All right then," I said as I tried to tie up the conversation. Eileen obviously felt comfortable with me, maybe too comfortable. She had revealed too much, which in this situation was a good thing for me. I knew she would not be getting the job. Eventually I led her to the door and said that I had more candidates to interview, but that I would be in touch with her either way.

I did call Eileen later to tell her that we had decided to go in another direction. She sounded genuinely disappointed and surprised, which frankly surprised me.

I conducted a few more phone screenings with candidates who saw my newspaper ad, but no one was promising. The candidates were either too young, too old, had no experience, wanted too many hours, didn't have enough hours to give me, and the list went on. I wondered why someone would answer my very short and to the point ad if they didn't meet those very minimum requirements.

"Well I can only work weekends," said one woman to me on the phone. Click.

"Can I bring my three children with me?" asked another. Click.

"I can't drive." Click.

And then I picked up a message on my home answering machine while out running errands one day. I was at the gas station and Joey was snug in his car seat, all zipped up in the fleece insert in the back of the car. I was getting a bit nervous that I couldn't go to work because I would have no one to watch my baby. I imagined never leaving Joey's side. Perhaps on his first day of kindergarten I could start to network? By that point though, I would be so far removed from the workplace environment that I would never be able to get back into it. And what about the next child? I'd have to wait until he or she started school too. My career was over.

Then I heard her voice on the machine.

"Hi, my name is Amy. I saw your ad in the paper about the nanny job, and I am interested. I just graduated from college, and I love taking care of babies. I have experience and references. Please call me back." She left her number.

I had a really good feeling about Amy. It was similar to the feeling I had after I first met with a young woman who I ended up hiring to work for me at Time Inc. in New York, and not too different from the sense I got after making a connection with my on-campus admissions interviewer at the University of Pennsylvania some thirteen years prior. Call it an instinct or just a strong feeling, but I've always been pretty perceptive. My mom taught me how to act on those feelings when I was nervous while prepping for the SATs way back in high school.

"Go with your gut feeling. . . . It's usually right," she used to say. I always had that voice in the back of my mind no matter what the situation.

I called Amy right back, and I liked the sound of her voice. She asked several good questions. I could tell she was serious about wanting the job and about proving to me that she would be good for it. She was a viable candidate and quite possibly the only viable one.

Amy came to our house for the face-to-face interview, and I liked her even more in person. She showed up wearing her oversized Penn State hooded sweatshirt and jeans. A bit casual, I thought, but comfy and ready to play with a baby. My first question to Amy sparked a good conversation, and I got to know some things about her and her family too. She had recently moved in with her parents after college, and she was taking graduate classes at night in education. She hoped to teach one day, and in the meantime, she needed a job and loved to be with children. It all sounded good to me.

I got excited as our conversation progressed, and I began to think that Amy was indeed the one. I started picturing her in our house, playing with Joey, feeding him, putting him down for a nap. I had to stop my over-active imagination and remind myself to play it cool.

"Would you like to see Joey's room?" I asked Amy, figuring we could talk more as I gave her a tour of his room and the rest of the house.

"Sure," she said with a smile as she carried Joey in her arms up our narrow and steep staircase. At that moment I was glad that we had the runner installed on the stairs, as I didn't want Amy to slip and fall, drop Joey, potentially hurt him, and then ruin my chance to hire her as our very first nanny. I made certain to show her Joey's favorite stuffed animal, Mr. Bear, and his cozy blanket, the one that had his full name, Joseph (which no one ever called him), sewn into both the light blue and white sides.

"This is where you would put him down for his nap, if you ended up working here of course," I explained as I tried not to get ahead of myself.

We ended up giving Amy the offer after she came back to meet Neil and my mother. Her references from past babysitting jobs were excellent. I gave her the specifics on the three full days of the week that I would need her to watch Joey. She agreed to that schedule and the hourly rate. I walked her through my expectations about showing up for work and showing up on time.

"After all," I reminded her. "When you can't come to work, then I can't go to work." She understood. We had successfully found and hired our first nanny. Nanny Amy worked out really well for two years until she had to leave us to find "a real job." At that point, I found myself wondering, *What are we?*

Rachel's Rules

NEWSPAPER ADS

The thing about searching for a nanny with a newspaper ad is that you need to be as specific as possible. You also need to screen really well over the phone. Everyone and their mother reads the want ads, especially in the local papers. You will end up spending more time than you care to interviewing "potential" nannies without a lot of potential if you don't phone screen first. Stacey's phone screening questions turned out to be an invaluable tool. If a candidate didn't have the right answers to the questions over the phone, then she didn't get an in-person interview.

Stacey's Nanny Screening Questions

Name:

Phone Number:

Availability:

Willing to take care of multiple children?

Prior Experience:

Where?

For who?

How long?

How many children?

Would you be able to provide these references?

Do you have a reliable form of transportation to/from my home?

When would you be able to start work?

It's also a good idea to have people that you know and trust meet the candidates in person like I did when interviewing nanny Amy with Neil and my mother. More people means more perspectives. Other people will not become as attached to candidates the way that the mother will. They are further removed from the situation. It was my mother who expressed concern about the shape of Amy's car. She wondered if it would be reliable enough to get her to and from our house. And she was right—several months into her time with us, Amy had car troubles.

The Online Ad

Our search for nanny number two was different from the first one, kind of like how baby number two is always different from baby number one. Not necessarily better or worse, just different. One of my new mom friends suggested that I place an ad on a local caregiving website. (I was so pleased to be making real connections with other moms in our new hometown. It was kind of like how I felt after I made real friends in college—not just the ones who lived on my freshman hall.) Searching for someone online to look after our then-toddler Joey and new baby girl on the way sounded a bit scary back in 2005. But my trusty new mom friends assured me that they had found great nannies online. It was certainly worth a shot.

The response to my online ad was overwhelming. The site generated an email to you every time someone answered your ad. I received so many that I had trouble focusing on work those first few days that the ad was posted. I felt kind of popular. I had met Neil before the days of online dating, but I imagined that this was in some way what it felt like to get lots of responses to your online dating profile. I figured we looked attractive to potential nannies. Perhaps we would have our pick of lots of qualified candidates?

The problem with an online ad, I soon learned, was that it was seen by so many people that so many responded whether they met the requirements or not—even more so than my initial ad in the paper that brought us nanny Amy. It was also springtime, and I was hearing from lots of college students who planned on being home for the summer, but were then headed right back to school come September. I assumed they could read the part of the ad that said "long-term permanent position." Apparently many candidates chose to ignore the fine print, albeit not so fine at all.

I had a great interview with one young woman named Catherine who came to me through the website. But by the time I responded to her inquiry, she had already taken another job—for my good friend Suzanne. Suzanne and I met when our first children were babies at a brunch hosted by a mutual friend. We hit it off right away, bonding over our pre-baby lives in New York City and our struggles to find good childcare so that we could hang on to our careers. Suzanne is a social worker who helps cancer patients through the physical and emotional roller coaster of their treatments. She also counsels grieving family members who have lost loved ones to the disease. Suzanne quickly became my unofficial therapist as we met just a few months after my mother died. I don't know what I would have done without her.

Almost instantly, I felt like I could tell Suzanne anything, and she later told me that the feeling was mutual. Our conversations flowed without effort as we discussed cancer and dying, friendship and family, and then easily switched gears to assembly instructions for baby bouncy seats and where to find the best salad dressings. Incidentally Suzanne makes the best salads and they always compliment my homemade desserts. We still talk about opening a restaurant one day where we would only serve salads and desserts.

Suzanne and I figured out pretty quickly one day that she had snatched nanny Catherine away from me off of the caregiving website as we compared notes. Catherine still babysits for Suzanne's children on Saturday nights, now nine years later. I sometimes wonder what would have happened if I had managed to get to Catherine and hire her as nanny number two. Would it have worked out? Would she still be our nanny today?

We ended up finding nanny number two, Ellie, from the same caregiving website. Ellie was an energetic and fun-loving young woman who already worked for another family two days a week and was able to work for us on the other three days. Ellie proposed the nanny share idea to us during the interview, and we thought it sounded great. Part-time work was ideal for my schedule, but it often made the nanny search more difficult as most candidates wanted full-time work. A nanny share made perfect sense to me.

Ellie had just earned her degree in elementary education, and she hoped to teach one day, but it was hard to get a teaching job, especially in the ultra-competitive school districts she was targeting. I figured one day she would make the leap from nanny to teacher, but I hoped that would not be for a long time. After all, that's what she had told us during the interview. She seemed bubbly and sweet, and she was great with then-two-year-old Joey. Ellie got right down on the floor and played with him, and we kind of fell in love. Until we fell out of love just four months later when Ellie left us to take a teaching job that she promised us she wouldn't take for at least another year.

My friend Nina found her fantastic first nanny of seven years from an ad she put on craigslist. I met Nina through our kids, who go to school together. Nina is a partner at a mid-sized law firm in downtown Philadelphia, and she is one of the best multitaskers I have ever met. She can make her three kids breakfast, do two loads of laundry, answer work emails, and prepare dinner for her nanny to warm up that evening, and all before 7:00 a.m. Her multitasking skills translate into her being a great friend, as she is always there to help me out, give my kids a ride, and bounce an idea off of. She also has great naturally curly hair, and I am probably most envious of that. After all, I was the kid who ate the crusts off of all my sandwiches because my mother told me it would give me curly hair. My hair is still pin straight, even on a really humid day.

Nina was looking for someone to watch her twin babies when they were just three months old. She had initially thought that she would put the twins in daycare, but chose to go the nanny route after negotiating a part-time work schedule with her firm. Nina felt a bit behind when she placed her nanny ad on craigslist just two weeks before going back to work. Luckily, she had a lot of responses to the ad, and she managed to screen over the phone until she narrowed down her pool to five candidates. Then two candidates canceled and two more didn't show up for their scheduled interviews. And then there was one—Liza.

As was the case with our first nanny, Amy, Liza seemed to be Nina's best hope, and most likely her only hope. Liza walked into Nina's house with a copy of the *New York Times* nicely tucked into an NPR tote bag, and Nina knew she was the one. She had to be. Looking back on that day, Nina now recognizes that she may have put a little too much faith into her intellectually snobby instinct, but it was something. If Liza read the paper of record ("All the News That's Fit to Print"), and listened to NPR enough to warrant carrying the actual tote bag around, then she had to be a good person to take care of her babies.

She was. Liza's interview went really well, as Nina and her husband Mark learned how Liza had retired from a teaching career in the Philadelphia public school system. She had raised three children of her own, one of whom went to college at Mark's Ivy League alma mater. If she had raised her kids to be happy and successful young adults, perhaps she would help to do the same for Nina and Mark's kids? Liza ended up being a very positive influence on their children. So much so that when the family moved out to the suburbs six years after hiring Liza, she continued to work for them for another full year. Eventually though, Liza needed more hours and the family needed fewer.

Nina's experience with nanny Liza was certainly better than my friend Lori's online recruitment from Care.com for her first nanny, Bonnie. Lori, then a New York–based accountant, was putting in the extra hours at her firm, even with a new baby at home. Lori felt that she couldn't get behind on her billable hours, especially as a new mother who was trying so hard to prove herself at the male-dominated firm where she worked. I admired her for doing this—for "leaning in" or "getting a seat at the table" (as much as those terms have become overused and have even started to annoy me). Lori was the real deal: a very impressive, young working mom. I wondered if I could have maintained the big corporate magazine job as a new mom. I was grateful for my part-time set-up at the smaller marketing firm.

Lori hired her nanny Bonnie contingent upon a few days of on-the-job training. During these few days, Lori worked from home to see how Bonnie did. It was a good thing Lori put that measure in place. Lori took a break from work in her home office and walked into her living room to check on baby Abby and nanny Bonnie. She found Bonnie sound asleep on the floor with her back against the couch, while Abby sat nearby and played with her plastic cup toys. Thankfully baby Abby was not yet mobile. Lori went back to Care.com and hired her second choice, who quickly rose to the ranks of first choice.

Rachel's Rules

ONLINE ADS

When you look for a nanny online, be prepared to act quickly. Otherwise you could lose out on a strong candidate like I did with Catherine. You should also be prepared to get those candidates who don't read that ever-important fine print. You know, the "fine print" that says you need part-time or full-time help, or someone that drives, or whatever essential thing it is that you need. When candidates go online, a lot of the time they are just browsing, and may respond to something on a whim without fully understanding the commitment. This was the case for our second nanny Ellie, who only worked for us for one summer. She probably always knew that it would be a summer fling.

The Nanny Agency

I had heard good things about nanny agencies. I felt like I needed someone else to qualify, or at least pre-qualify, candidates in our search for nanny number three after nanny Ellie left so suddenly. I was really busy with work, taking care of a toddler, and feeling not so great as I was then further along in my second pregnancy. I hoped that an agency's background checks would weed out those nannies that only wanted to be a nanny for the short-term.

I found a local nanny agency and went to the office to meet the staff in person. I was determined to find someone good, and someone who would be committed to being our nanny for a while. Somehow I thought a face-to-face meeting would help. The agency staff consisted of one person: the owner, an ambitious and friendly woman named Patty who was trying hard to build a business. She saw the need for this kind of service in our area. I obviously did too.

Patty's office was filled with pictures of nannies and the families she had placed them with, as well as caregivers she had placed with elderly clients. I was willing to give her a chance. I agreed to the terms of her services, which included a $2,000 placement fee that guaranteed a nanny for us for one year. I waited to hear back from her with a slew of qualified candidates. I managed to squeeze in some résumé screenings at work via email, and then forwarded them to Neil at his office. Nothing was very promising, until the call one day from Patty with a woman who she described as a "dream nanny." She was a young woman named Molly who Patty had placed years ago with a family that was very happy with her. The only reason Molly was leaving the family was because they no longer needed her as the children had outgrown needing a nanny.

That sounded amazing to me. I imagined this magical Molly caring for our children until we outgrew her. Molly had moved to the United States from Russia when she was a little girl, and she had a very strong work ethic, as explained to me by Patty and also by the family she was working for. In addition to keeping on top of the kids to get their homework done, Molly also kept the house extremely neat and always went the extra mile to make sure things got done properly.

Neil and I could picture all these things to be true about Molly when we met and eventually hired her. It was a bigger commitment for us this time as we were paying a pretty hefty agency fee to Patty and paying Molly more than our past nannies ($14 per hour versus $12 per hour). But, we reminded ourselves, Molly had more qualifications and seemed to us to be a career nanny, whatever that meant. She was happy to work for us three days a week, and Patty found her work cleaning houses for the other two days. It was a done deal. And it worked for about a year until Molly became unexpectedly pregnant, and we were left unexpectedly without a nanny once again.

Nannies number four and five also came to us through Patty's agency. Nanny number four, Julie, looked good on paper. She was a young woman with lots of babysitting experience and glowing references from several families. She lived at home with her parents nearby, and was babysitting on and off. She had no plans to go to college, as she told us that she wanted to be a "lifelong nanny."

Julie seemed great when we interviewed her, although one of her answers did strike me as a bit strange. When I asked her one of my standard questions, "What are you most proud of?" she explained that she was most proud of losing a tremendous amount of weight in recent years. I couldn't imagine her being heavy, as she was a really tiny young woman. But I went with it. Good for her. It showed willpower and determination to lose as much weight as she said she had. We hired her. I later discovered that Julie had been a bulimic for years. She had to stop working for us just six months later when she ended up in the hospital after passing out from taking too many diet pills.

Patty from the agency then came to me with nanny number five, Alice, an older and experienced nanny who had been with her last family for almost five years. According to Patty, Alice was looking for a new job because the family she was working for was moving down to Virginia to be closer to their extended family. Alice was also specifically looking for part-time work, as she wanted a couple of days a week to be with her grandchildren. It sounded promising.

Alice came to meet us on a cold Saturday afternoon, and my dad was at our house to act as another set of eyes. I still felt that the more people who met her and could give me an opinion on her, the better. I was starting to doubt my own judgment. I had hired and held on to so many great people to work for me back at the magazine company in New York. Why couldn't I manage to find and hold on to a good nanny? Could anyone?

My father, Neil, and I were all impressed with Alice. She offered advice right away during the interview on why our baby Rebecca wasn't yet crawling. Alice explained how she would get Rebecca up and moving in no time at all. Apparently the previous nanny, Julie, had held Rebecca too much and had not given her enough tummy (or as Neil called it, torture) time. Alice had raised four kids of her own, helped out with even more grandchildren, and nannied for numerous families over the years. She even went to nursing school and knew a fair bit about healthcare as it related to children. Alice ended up being our longest-term nanny, coming in at just shy of three years.

Ellen, a close friend of mine since childhood, searched for and eventually found her second nanny through an agency. Ellen and I had met each other when we were still in our own cribs, or so the story went. Ellen's mother called my mother in the spring of 1974, right after Ellen was born, as she had heard that my mother had a great baby nurse that helped to care for me, and Ellen's mother wanted to hire the same nurse for baby Ellen. From that point on, our lives were forever connected. Ellen and I grew up down the street from each other, took ballet lessons together, joined the same brownie troop, and even shared a flat in London as college students studying abroad during our junior year. Ellen and I still talk at least once a week during her morning commute. She hasn't taken much to email and texting as a way to stay in touch, and I am good with that. Ellen has always been a real phone person, even when, as a teenager, her time on the phone was limited after the dermatologist told her that all those hours on the phone with me and other friends were causing her chin and lower cheek to break out. I sometimes remind her of that during our longer chats, and she tells me she is happy with the development of the hands-free phone.

During one of those phone conversations, I referred Ellen to a few nanny agencies in New Jersey where she lived with her husband Rob, her one-year-old daughter Natalie, and a baby boy on the way. Ellen's children would be fourteen months apart, much closer than she had ever imagined, but Ellen had fertility issues, and after trying for years for her first child, Ellen became pregnant with baby number two rather quickly. It was a really good surprise.

Ellen commuted about an hour and a half each way to her office in New Jersey where she worked as a human resources consultant. She needed a nanny who could give her a lot of hours because of her long days. She explained this to the agency, and when the agency sent nanny Franny to Ellen's front porch with her Welsh accent and soft yellow Fair Isle sweater, Ellen fell in love. Ellen thought she had found her very own Mary Poppins. During the interview, Franny explained to Ellen how she would wear a different colored shirt or sweater every day to teach her baby about all the different colors. Franny was also big on manners and assured Ellen that her baby would be saying please and thank you, even before mama and no.

Ellen hired nanny Franny after reviewing her glowing references and excellent background check provided by the agency. She agreed to the agency's terms. In this case, the agency guaranteed Ellen one and half years of service after she paid them 15 percent of Franny's annual salary. Franny continues to work for Ellen now some two years after being placed with her, and although she is not the Mary Poppins Ellen had initially envisioned, she works for them . . . for now.

Rachel's Rules

NANNY AGENCIES

I thought a nanny agency would be the answer to all of my prayers—that they would do all the background checks, provide references, and screen for my specific needs. They did do that to an extent, but you still have to do your own work. You have to make sure the candidates they give you are the right fit for your own needs. The candidates may look good on paper, but they have to be good in your home and with your children. Agencies are also getting a lot of the same candidates that are responding to your own ads on Care.com, craigslist, and other websites. In fact, many of the agencies advertise on these sites to get their candidates. They do not pull from some magical list of perfect nannies, so don't expect the candidates to be all that different from the ones you could find on your own.

Word of Mouth

We found some of our best nannies through word of mouth. Nanny number six, Madeline, came to us because she worked at the babysitting club at our local gym. She heard me ask the front desk manager if he knew of anyone at the gym who was good with kids and wanted to watch two children after school. At that point, our kids were old enough not to need an all-day nanny. Madeline approached me a few days later as I was rushing to get in twenty minutes on the elliptical machine at the gym. She asked if I still needed help, and I replied that I did. She ended up watching our kids in the afternoons for about a year and a half, and still babysits for us on Saturday nights.

When Madeline had to leave us during the afternoons because of an overloaded college class schedule, she provided us with a new nanny: April. April had actually worked for my friend and nanny-finding boss Stacey as an everyday afternoon sitter, but over time could only work three days a week, which didn't work for Stacey. It was perfect for us. Madeline and April got to know each other from carpooling our kids around, and brokered the deal without me even knowing about it. I liked that Madeline took the initiative. April watched our kids after school for two years.

Stacey had initially used word of mouth to find April, as April went to school with a woman who worked for Stacey in her office. I still keep up with a few of Stacey's former nannies as they have referred me to friends of theirs that have worked as babysitters and nannies for me and for many of my friends. It seems as though we know their whole network of part-time nanny friends, right down to their college class schedules, internships, and even their boyfriends.

Suzanne, my friend the social worker and unofficial grief counselor, used word of mouth to find her awesome first nanny by asking around at the local preschool. So did Janie, another mom friend of mine, and a work from home marketing manager. Janie has employed the sister-in-law of her childrens' teacher for over two years. All she had to do was ask around the hallways of the school, and she found someone great. And my friend Anne, a pharmaceutical executive and mother of three young children (and whose middle daughter has been mistaken on more than one occasion as a twin for my daughter Rebecca), found her excellent nanny of four years after her husband asked around the barbershop. It turned out that the barber had a customer whose wife was a teacher and was looking to become a nanny.

Rachel's Rules

WORD OF MOUTH

Word of mouth can be a great way to find a nanny. You are removing a bit of the unknown factor when you work through your own network of family, friends, and colleagues. People who know you will generally refer people that they know or at least suspect will fit well with your family and meet your family's needs. It can get tricky though, if it doesn't work out with someone referred to you by someone you know. You also need to be very proactive when using word of mouth to find a nanny. Ask everywhere you can—even at the barbershop! You never know who will know of a good nanny.

2

To Live-In or Not to Live-In

When I was a child, our across-the-street neighbors and very good friends had a live-in nanny named Wendy. Wendy was a godsend for the family. She lived upstairs, down the hall from the two young girls, who were right around my age, and she had her own room and bathroom. Wendy took care of the girls and me whenever I was over there, which was a lot when their mother was at work and their father was away on business trips.

Wendy was the ideal live-in nanny. She ran the house like no one else, drove the girls around to wherever they needed to be, fit in so easily with the family, and she made the most amazing lemon bars. The girls tried to replicate her lemon bars after they had grown up and Wendy had moved out, but they never could. It would be nice if everyone could find a live-in situation like that, but it can be very difficult to make it work. I found that out pretty quickly. And so too did my childhood neighbors. When the kids went off to college and the parents got divorced, nanny Wendy professed her love to the dad. The feeling was not mutual. Nanny Wendy left very quickly with her lemon bar recipe and all.

Live-In

Neil and I never had anyone live with us except, well, us. That was until we had kids. Right after Joey was born, we employed a baby nurse named Jackie who lived with us for three weeks. Jackie was originally from Trinidad and shared an apartment in Brooklyn with a few of her baby nurse friends so they had a place to stay when they weren't working on a case.

My mother, who was fighting her way through the metastatic tumors in her liver and what would be the last few months of her life, had arranged for Jackie to come live with us right after I came home from the hospital with Joey. I had heard of baby nurses before, mostly anecdotal tales from friends and from my mother and Ellen's mother, who always marveled at how great our baby nurse was way back when. I questioned my mother numerous times on the necessity of having this extra help with only one new baby to care for, but my mother insisted on getting a nurse. She even offered to pay Jackie for the time she was with us. I think my mother felt a little bit sorry for me because she was so sick and was unable to help with my new baby. I decided not to look a gift horse in the mouth, and so arrived Jackie.

She came in through our kitchen door with a big smile on her face, and that smile never went away for the three weeks that she lived with us. Jackie loved babies, especially tiny newborns. It seemed as though she had chosen the right line of work. She got right down to business as she took baby Joey from my arms and swaddled him so quickly and tightly. He looked like a perfect little package. I was amazed. I didn't know what had hit us.

I wanted to make sure Jackie felt comfortable in our home and asked her what types of foods she wanted us to get for her. She insisted that she wouldn't need a thing as she was strictly following the Slimfast diet. Jackie came fully equipped with containers of powder for the shakes. I kind of wondered how long a person could live only on Slimfast. I soon found out that it wasn't too long.

Our second night at home together, my mother's sister, who is a wonderful cook, delivered a homemade meal of meatloaf, potatoes, Caesar salad, fresh bread, and even her famous home-baked chocolate chunk cookies (the ones that I liked to store in, and then eat right out of, the freezer). Jackie took one look at the meal, and the Slimfast containers would not be opened for the rest of her stay. She very quickly put herself on the Lesser family meal plan.

I didn't blame her for it either. We had great food during those first few weeks of parenthood, and I kind of thought that Jackie could appreciate a good meal. She was a large woman with a large appetite for our delicious homemade meals, and as I would soon come to understand, an even larger appetite for life. Jackie soaked it all in and enjoyed every minute of it.

I really liked our dinnertime together as a newly formed, if somewhat odd, family. Jackie and I would wait for Neil to get home from work, then sit down to whatever I'd get out of the freezer from the extended family-made meals. Baby Joey would either lie in the bassinet next to me or sometimes in my arms. I truly enjoyed Jackie's company as I adjusted to motherhood.

Neil felt otherwise. He was ready for Jackie to go after just the first week. He did not find her scheduled viewing of *Jeopardy* on the family television every night, along with the calling out of all the answers, or rather questions, in the middle of our conversations as amusing as I did. I'll admit that having someone who is not related to you live with you can be challenging. I think Neil came to understand this more quickly than I did. He knew that even after I did go back to work, we would not have a nanny live with us.

Neil drew the line after one evening in which he drove Jackie to the Sprint store to pay her phone bill, then to CVS where he bought her a special mesh laundry bag that she could wash her bras in, and then to the Western Union where she wired money home to her family in Trinidad. I got it. Having someone live with you to help with childcare can be problematic. In some ways you end up taking care of that person's needs. Especially if, as was the case with Jackie, that person can't drive. In some ways, it's like having another child.

When Jackie left, I knew it was time. She had brought out her cousin Barbara from Brooklyn for her last few days with us, as she was training Barbara to be a baby nurse and nanny. There were way too many people in our house at that point. Someone had to go.

Years later, Jackie's cousin, Barbara, became the live-in and first nanny for my childhood friend Ellen in New Jersey. Initially Ellen thought that her long commute and even longer work hours required her to hire a live-in nanny. She and her husband Rob ran the numbers and figured it would be most economical to hire someone to live with them. They calculated a savings of close to $1,000 per month by having a nanny live with them instead of live out. They later learned that there were other out-of-pocket costs that they hadn't fully considered. Things like paying for Barbara's groceries and for cable television for her room.

Although the cable costs added up, Ellen knew that it was well worth it. Cable television for nanny Barbara gave her and Rob some quiet time together at night after a long day at work, and with baby Natalie fast asleep. Ellen and Rob had a pretty good set-up for Barbara, since they only had one baby at the time. Barbara slept in what was supposed to be the guest room upstairs, which was close to the baby's room, and she had her own bathroom. She also did baby Natalie's laundry, and when she had time, she did Ellen and Rob's as well.

Ellen hadn't really thought too much about dinnertime with Barbara, and it turned out she didn't have to. Starting on day one, Barbara sat down to dinner with Ellen and Rob. This happened every night—even when baby Natalie had already gone to sleep. Ellen didn't expect it to be like this, but she didn't want to offend nanny Barbara, and so she never said anything. Ellen loved to cook and always considered herself a pretty good cook, but apparently nanny Barbara thought otherwise. This became apparent when nanny Barbara stopped eating Ellen's food and offered to cook dinner for the family. Again, not wanting to offend nanny Barbara, Ellen went along with the plan and told Rob that he would be eating Barbara's cooking too, whether he liked it or not.

And so Ellen and Rob learned the ins and outs of traditional Trinidadian food. They liked the spices but weren't thrilled with the Carnation brand canned evaporated milk that complimented each meal, no matter what the main ingredient was. Barbara worked for Ellen and Rob for six months, until Ellen became pregnant with baby number two. A new baby meant no more room for a live-in nanny. It was time to move on. The cable was taken out of Barbara's room, and in place of the television stand went a second crib.

Lori, the New York–based accountant who didn't have such great luck with her first trial nanny Bonnie (who fell asleep on the floor), eventually hired a live-in nanny. Lori and her husband Steve moved with their two little girls to the Philadelphia suburbs to be near extended family on both sides. Lori figured that having extra family around would be helpful to her with her work schedule. She negotiated with her firm so that she could work out of her home office, and then travel to New York or wherever she was needed for in-person meetings.

Lori and Steve had a seemingly great set-up in their basement for their second nanny, Tricia. The walkout basement provided nanny Tricia with her own entrance, so she could come and go as she pleased during her time off. Yet Tricia always came in and out of the main floor entrance. Nanny Tricia had her own room, her own bathroom, and use of the large television and cozy couches downstairs to watch whatever she wanted to at night, but she rarely did that. Much like nanny Barbara did with Ellen's family, nanny Tricia chose to spend more time with the family than was required of her, and she was required to spend a lot of time on nanny duty.

Lori had taken on a larger role in her accounting firm when she and Steve hired Tricia to care for their girls. Like Ellen, Lori worked long hours. And although she was able to work from home, she traveled more often than not. A live-in nanny was really a necessity for Lori, especially with her husband's long commute. Tricia drove to Lori and Steve's house every Sunday night from her parents' home about an hour away, where she lived on the weekends. She headed back to her parents' house every Friday evening. Tricia has worked for the family for five plus years, but her role changed as the girls were in school more and more. She was a nanny and caretaker to the kids, and when they were in school, she was a home manager. Tricia grocery shopped, picked up the family dry cleaning, bought presents for the girls' friends' birthday parties, and took the cat to the vet. She did it all. Lori would have been lost without Tricia, and she was so grateful to have her. But that didn't mean that it was a perfect set-up. Far from it.

When Lori wasn't traveling, she worked from her house in the home office right next to Tricia's bedroom in the basement. That worked well when Tricia was out and about driving the kids to school and running family errands, but when she was home doing laundry in the basement, it got tricky. Lori had to take too many work calls from the floor of the walk-in closet in her bedroom upstairs in order to keep up the appearance (at least over the phone) of a professional work environment. She found herself hiding from her own nanny on many occasions, not wanting to have her work day interrupted by questions and comments about the girls' schedules and their homework habits, which were becoming an issue.

Tricia helped the girls with their homework, which shouldn't have been too time consuming given their young ages, but there were times when Tricia didn't quite get it. Lori had to get involved, but she really didn't have the time for it. After all, that's why she had hired a live-in nanny—to have someone on call for homework and other things that she couldn't be available for as she was working on building her client list. Lori didn't really have a choice though. She had to get involved or the homework wouldn't get finished. Or it would get finished but with too many mistakes. Lori eventually found a happy medium by having her mother, a retired school teacher who lived nearby, come over to help out when the homework was too tough for nanny Tricia.

Although Lori knew that she needed nanny Tricia to live in the house to make her family's life run relatively smoothly, she also secretly wished that Tricia would disappear when the workday was done. Nanny Tricia never did. Tricia fed Lori's kids their dinner, and then Lori would come upstairs from her office in the basement to take over. Tricia wasn't so great about letting Lori do this. Nanny Tricia often lingered in the kitchen, and then the family room, until the children went to bed. She sat with the family as they watched television at night, and made comments about the day's events, offering unsolicited parenting advice to Lori. By that time in the day, Lori just wanted to be with her kids, and her husband if he made it home before the girls' bedtime.

As was the case with Ellen and nanny Barbara, Lori did not want to offend nanny Tricia or rock the boat, because the situation worked well for them in so many other ways. Eventually, though, Lori did say something because she couldn't take it anymore. Lori talked to her nanny about the need to have their own family time in the evenings, but she was never sure that Tricia ever fully got it. Every once in a while, Lori would stop working early enough to get the girls together to go out for a special weeknight dinner, and Tricia always assumed she was included. Lori didn't feel that she could leave her out. So the family went out to dinner: Lori, sometimes Steve, the girls, and nanny Tricia. It was their weekday family. They did what they had to do to make it work as best as they could for as long as they could.

Rachel's Rules

One of the keys to a good live-in nanny situation is having the right set-up. That means having good space in your home to provide some privacy for both the family and the nanny. Whether it's a room for your nanny on a separate floor with her own bathroom and television, or whatever. Give her space and hopefully she will do the same for you for those off-duty hours. But you also have to be clear about that space and that time. This was often hard for Ellen and Lori to do. That's understandable, and a mistake that many working mothers make. You are employing someone to care for your children, hopefully in the way that you would care for them yourself. So there is a fine line there. You don't want to cross it by offending your nanny, but you have to be up-front. Explain that when you come home from work, you are the one in charge, and that your family needs some family time alone.

You also need to have a certain temperament to successfully employ a live-in nanny. I clearly did not have that temperament. I was always making sure everyone was taken care of, even if that person was working for me. I ended up spending a significant amount of time helping Jackie with her computer (she always had trouble connecting to our network) and taking her to Starbucks for her decaf extra hot skim latte. My mother had a similar temperament, and she told me a story about the time she brought a nanny away with us on our family vacation. The nanny had a great vacation as my mother did all her laundry and served her meals. It's important to remember that your nanny can take care of herself. After all, you are paying her to take care of other people, so assume she can manage her own needs. Chances are, if she wants something from you, she will ask.

Live-Out

Live-out nannies worked better for us. Once we had two children, we had no room to squeeze anyone else into our house, and we liked having the house to ourselves at the end of the day. All of our nannies were pretty good with the evening transitions. I'd come home to get the daily report from nanny number one, Amy, who recorded Joey's napping and eating schedule in a notebook along with any phone messages. I never asked her to do that, but I liked that she did. She wasn't the best in-person communicator. Writing things down worked better for her.

Nanny number five, Alice, loved to make an early dinner for our kids. She made sure the children were fed and the kitchen was all cleaned up before I came home. She spent a few minutes with me telling me about her day with the kids, and that was it. I was in charge. Nanny Alice knew it, the kids knew it, and so did I. I liked those clear lines, especially after a long day at work.

Our fourth nanny, Julie, didn't always leave so quickly after I came home from work. She often got caught up in telling me her own personal stories, including the latest drama with her boyfriend. I tried to listen as best as I could when all I really wanted to do was be with my children and get on with the night. I regularly reminded myself that this water cooler talk was important, especially for the person whose job it was to care for my children.

There were a few occasions when nanny Julie was late in getting to our house in the morning because of traffic or an accident or a bad blow dryer, and then I was late for work. Those were the times when I learned that having a live-out nanny can be problematic. Live-out nannies have to get to your house, and if they can't be there when you need them to be, it can throw off your whole day. It was hard enough for me to get ready for work and find a shirt without a spit-up stain on my right shoulder. When I did manage to pick out a shirt that stayed clean all morning, I really hoped nanny Julie would show up on time.

Nanny Alice was always on time, if not early, in the morning. She liked to get to our house to make herself her own elaborate breakfast. Sometimes she cooked an omelet, or sometimes pancakes with a side of fruit. By that point, nanny Alice was doing a lot of the grocery shopping, so I was happy that she had found things that she liked to eat. Her cooking for herself at our house didn't bother me, even if our kitchen smelled like an IHOP most mornings. I think our endless supply of food and large cooktop motivated Alice to get to work on time, and that made my life easier. Whatever it took, I told myself.

Rachel's Rules

LIVE-OUT

When I look back on our various nanny situations, I think that it might have made more economic sense for us to have hired a live-in nanny, especially early on when the kids were little. We paid our nannies on an hourly basis for their time with us, and we gave them gas money to drive the kids around and to get to and from our house. Because Neil worked long hours and traveled a lot, I would on occasion get a weeknight sitter if I had to be somewhere for work late. We also paid for a Saturday night sitter and a housekeeper. If we did go the live-in route, we probably would have saved money by giving all of those jobs to one person, and not necessarily paying by the hour. My childhood friend Ellen figured that out with nanny Barbara early on.

It didn't matter though, because after baby nurse Jackie, we knew that live-out worked best for us. It is so important to know what works for your family, and this may take some trial and error. If it ends up being a live-out situation, make sure you are clear on expectations up-front. Tell your nanny exactly when she needs to be at your house in the morning, and set out a plan for a nightly transition to pass the proverbial torch from nanny to parent. It may even help to write out a contract with explicit rules and expectations regarding punctuality and days off. Communication is always key.

～ 3 ～

Country Mouse, City Mouse

I grew up in a very countrified suburb of Philadelphia. It's a beautiful town with a quaint main street straight out of a Norman Rockwell painting—old colonial homes and still untouched farmland further away from town. I had a great childhood, even if I thought it was kind of boring. I always thought that I would live in the city when I grew up, and so my parents were quite surprised when I told them that I was moving back to suburban Philadelphia after graduate school.

I had gone to college in Philadelphia, and after graduation I had moved right to New York City, then on to graduate school in Michigan, wanting to get as far away from my boring little childhood suburb as I could. But when I became pregnant in grad school, I realized that my little countrified suburban town and the surrounding areas were pretty great places to grow up. Neil did too. And he was pleased to get the good job offer in his firm's Philadelphia office after business school. He saw it as an opportunity to become a big fish in a small pond and develop a new area of expertise in consulting. By then, we knew that we didn't want to raise children in a city, and my mother was getting sicker and sicker by the month. I was more certain than ever that I should be near her for whatever amount of time she had left. So back to Pennsylvania I went with my husband and very large pregnant belly.

The Suburban Nanny

Neil and I had a bit of an adjustment to life in the burbs, as we hadn't spent any significant amount of time there since we were kids. Neil had grown up in a somewhat similar suburb to my childhood, one just north of New York City. We suddenly found ourselves with a suburban home, two suburban cars, a suburban baby, and a suburban nanny.

I learned that in some ways looking for a nanny in the burbs can be more difficult than looking in the city. While the suburban nanny search wasn't as competitive as the city nanny search, it really was a numbers game and a lesson in economics. There was more demand in the city and therefore more supply. When I went the nanny agency route, one city agency, The Philadelphia Nanny Network, found several extremely qualified candidates for me. But by the time the Philadelphia nanny candidates made it out to our house for the interview, they realized that they couldn't make the hour-long plus commute with traffic work. I did too. It just didn't make any sense.

The Driving Nanny

All of our nannies lived in nearby towns, they had their driver's licenses, and they drove our kids around—a lot. Driving is a big part of the job for suburban nannies, especially as the kids get older. Nanny number five, Alice, seemed like a caretaker and chauffeur to our children.

When both of our kids were in preschool, nanny Alice drove them to and from school and to friends' houses for play dates. She also ran errands for our family when the kids were in school. Alice was a good driver, and even better, she had a minivan. My kids liked her car set-up much better than my SUV, and so did I.

Nanny number one Amy had a smaller car, but she only drove Joey around in the days before Rebecca was born. She did have a funny habit of parking her car in all different parts of our narrow driveway. That wasn't usually a problem until the day I was flustered by the thought of an upcoming stressful meeting awaiting me at work. I backed out of my spot in the garage and plowed into her car, which was for some reason parked directly behind mine that day. The accident was clearly my fault, and I took full responsibility. Nanny Amy downplayed the situation.

"Just let me know how much the damage is, and I'll pay for it—all of it," I explained.

"It's okay Rachel," Amy said. "I bet my boyfriend can just bump it out or I can put a big Penn State sticker on the back door and no one will ever notice it."

I didn't know if she could ever open her back door again. It occurred to me then that our nanny didn't want to rock the boat either. She too knew that it was a unique situation and a delicate relationship between nanny and mother. If some stranger had backed into her car like that in a parking lot, I'm not so sure she would have been as forgiving. I paid for the repairs and managed not to hit her car again.

Driving became an issue for my friend Stacey's fourth nanny, Gina. While Stacey worked in marketing and business development for her family's business, her husband Phil worked from home for a tech company based in California. Although Phil was home for most of the day, he was on conference calls, locked in their upstairs home office. Stacey kept nanny Gina very busy driving their three boys to all of their after-school activities and sports practices. Nanny Gina seemed to be a very responsible driver, until Gina called one Sunday evening with bad news.

"I was in an accident over the weekend," reported Gina.

"Oh no," said Stacey very concerned. "Are you okay?" she asked.

"I'm a little banged up, but I got a DUI. It was pretty bad, and my license was taken away from me temporarily. I'm so so sorry, but I promise I will make it work," Gina explained further.

Stacey was less than thrilled with the report and wondered what to do. After a lengthy discussion with Phil, they decided to give Gina a chance and see what options she could come up with. Despite the DUI, they really liked Gina and so did the boys. Nanny Gina had worked well for their family for nearly three years. They knew that they had every right to fire her. After all, the DUI showed really poor judgment, and Gina was no longer able to fulfill one of her key job responsibilities: driving. But for Stacey, like so many other working moms I know, searching for a new nanny sounded so much more daunting.

Gina figured out a way to get rides to and from Stacey's house every day. And Stacey found rides for her children to and from their after school activities from neighbors and other carpoolers. It was a temporary solution that got them through that tricky three-month period of employing a suburban nanny who couldn't drive.

My friend Suzanne, the social worker, loved her suburban nanny Rori, but she often worried about Rori driving her kids around town. In fact, when Suzanne hired her first nanny years before with just one baby at home, she never thought her nanny would drive her baby anywhere. Suzanne just couldn't imagine giving someone else that big of a responsibility with her own child. As her baby got older and she had another one, she could see that the nanny would have to drive her children around. It was simply a necessity of living in the burbs.

Nanny Rori had an old two-door car that wasn't in great shape. Suzanne didn't want to discriminate based on what type of car her nanny drove. She would never have done that in other aspects of her life, and especially in her field of social work, where she got paid to be extra understanding and sympathetic. Still, Suzanne felt bad for her kids when they were squeezed in the small backseat of Rori's car. The kids didn't seem to mind, and Suzanne learned to live with it. Suzanne thought about giving her car to nanny Rori to drive the kids around, but Suzanne had a fairly long commute, and she didn't want to get stuck driving Rori's car. Suzanne recognized the absurdity of her conundrum: it was fine for her kids to ride in nanny Rori's less-than-appealing car, but it was not good enough for her. When Rori had car trouble, and she did, a lot, she managed to get rides to and from work from her boyfriend. Sometimes she borrowed his car. Suzanne and her kids liked those days, as the boyfriend's car was in better shape and had four doors.

Beyond the driving issue though, Suzanne always felt that she could never find a real career nanny like her friends from college employed in New York City. I knew what she meant. Suzanne's nannies always seemed less together and less professional. She couldn't always put her finger on it, but it was there. Suzanne and her husband Scott had made a conscious decision to leave the city even before they had kids, and they were happy with their decision. So many aspects of suburban life were easier for them with kids, but the nanny situation . . . maybe not so much.

The City Nanny

I got my initial sneak peak into city nanny life from my childless days of living and working in New York City. As I walked to work every day, I saw packs of nannies walking down the sidewalk together, pushing babies in single and double strollers, or sometimes holding the hand of a small child who they cared for. It was like this whole little underground world that I knew nothing about. I was intrigued, and I learned more as my friends became parents in the city.

My good friend from college, Jane, and her husband Evan, decided to stay in the city after they had children. They loved city life, and they didn't want to make their commutes longer by moving to the burbs. Jane was a city girl. I knew this when I met her back in college in Philadelphia. Jane was the most put-together college student I had ever seen. I used to take note of her sophisticated outfits that she donned for our 9:00 a.m. history class. Jane was the only girl in the morning recitation who, on a Friday, wore slacks. Everyone else just showed up in jeans or sweats. Jane later told me that she took note of the observations that I shared with our Recent American History class on the Cuban Missile Crisis. I was flattered that the fashion maven liked what I had to say.

After admiring each other from afar in class, we became close when we shared a house with several other girls during our junior year. I soon learned what a good person and devoted friend Jane would become. She helped me move all of my furniture up from the basement in our shared house, even though we were just getting to know each other. Jane always did the right thing. She was a strict follower of Emily Post's rules on etiquette, and she truly believed in them. She wrote a thank you note for everything. I swear she once wrote me a thank you note for a thank you note that I had sent her.

After college, Jane worked in fashion in New York City, and then in the arts as the director of a well-known museum's retail store. Jane and Evan had plenty of space in their apartment for a crib for their first child, a baby girl named Helena. They just needed a nanny so that Jane could go back to work at the museum store, where she had been employed for over a decade. Jane was amazed at the competitive business of finding and hiring a nanny in the city.

"If you want to find a good nanny in the city, you need to be ready to act fast," explained Jane to me one day over coffee.

She learned this the hard way after she interviewed a strong candidate referred to her by a work colleague. Jane and Evan really liked this one nanny, and called her references soon after meeting with her. Twenty-four hours later, Jane called the nanny to offer her the job, but it was too late. In the time it took Jane to check references, the nanny had taken an offer from another family. Jane couldn't believe it. She had never had a candidate snatched away from her like that in all her years working for the museum store. At the very least, the nanny could have called her to check in before she took the other job, Jane thought. It was a tough business.

Jane and Evan forged on and found another nanny candidate whom they both really liked. This candidate was working temporarily and on a part-time basis for another family where the father was a very popular New York City newscaster. In fact, Jane watched this newscaster on television every morning while she got ready for work. Jane thought this to be a funny coincidence, and was just a little bit excited to hire the nanny of a local celebrity. After Jane and Evan offered the job to newscaster nanny, she informed them that the temporary family had offered her a full-time and permanent job, and she had taken it. Jane realized that the nanny must have used Jane as leverage to go back to the other family. Whatever the case was, Jane and Evan had been jilted again. Jane stopped watching her once-favorite newscaster, now turned nanny stealer.

When Jane met a third strong nanny candidate named Lily, she knew that she had to act fast or she would lose out once again. Evan was out of town on business, and so Jane's mother came over to meet Lily. Jane and her mother loved everything about Lily. She seemed extremely professional and also very loving and caring with baby Helena. Jane and her mother knew Lily was a winner. Lily hadn't even made it down the elevator into the lobby before Jane called her on her cell phone to offer her the job. Jane hired Lily without her even meeting Evan, and without checking references (which she did later on), because she had been burned before. Jane was getting a sense of how nanny life worked in the city.

Lily still works for Jane and her family, now almost four years later, caring for little girl Helena and baby boy

Oscar. As Jane suspected, Lily was as professional as she had imagined she would be from day one. Lily is originally from the Philippines, and made lots of nanny friends from her years of working for other families in the city. Many of her nanny friends are also from the Philippines, and she explained to Jane how the packs of nannies, the same ones I used to see walking down the street when I lived in the city, often stuck together by culture and by countries of origin.

Jane and Lily became very close over the years, and Lily explained the pecking order within the world of New York City nannies to Jane. Those who had lots of experience and worked for families with multiple children made more money than those just starting out caring for one child. That made sense to Jane. City nannies, just like professionals in other fields, had to work their way up the corporate, or in this case, the nanny ladder. When Lily started working for Jane and Evan caring for just baby Helena, she made $15 an hour. That was about the starting point for most nannies in the city. In the suburbs, the starting rate is lower, at about $12 an hour.

In the city, there are very clear lines and rules about promotions and increases in pay. When another child comes along, the nanny's rate goes up by 20 percent. An experienced nanny in the city working for a family with three children will earn a lot more than a suburban nanny—up to $20 an hour in the city, versus $12–$15 an hour in the suburbs. Most city nannies also require a car service ride home if they are watching the children late into the night. Those costs can add up very quickly. I never employed a nanny who asked for a raise when another child came along. There wasn't a clearly defined business model like that in the burbs.

Over the years, Jane made her own friends through nanny Lily. Lily had her regular playgrounds, parks, and classes where she went with Helena and Oscar to meet up with her nanny friends and the children they cared for. Helena and Oscar had instant playmates in these other children. Jane always marveled at the other life that her children lived. Sometimes on the weekends, Jane would get to infiltrate part of that world and get her kids together with their weekday friends and meet their mothers, a few of whom she befriended. Jane realized that her nanny had become a matchmaker of sorts for her, and that was great for Jane's social life.

Nannies in the city are also bonded together by neighborhood. In New York, the downtown nannies go to Washington Square Park, and the uptown nannies go to Central Park. The Upper West Side nannies take the children to the American Museum of Natural History, and the Upper East Side nannies go to The Metropolitan Museum of Art. It would be very hard for an Upper East Side nanny to spend time with a Brooklyn nanny. The logistics just wouldn't work.

While Jane had total confidence in nanny Lily, she still worried about someone other than herself taking her kids out and about in the city. While driving is not an issue in the city like it is in the suburbs, Jane got nervous about Lily losing her kids on the crowded playgrounds or losing control of the oversized double stroller in traffic. City nannies take kids out of the apartments much more than suburban nannies do with their kids. Part of it is a real estate issue. City apartments are, for the most part, smaller than suburban houses. The kids need to get out more. In many ways it's easier for city nannies to go out and about in their neighborhood with the kids than it is for suburban nannies to venture out in cars with car seats. The stroller becomes the preferred method of transportation for city nannies, and some city strollers are ready for all the elements with oversized tires and retractable rain shields. A city stroller would have taken down my Maclaren suburban stroller any day of the week.

My good friend Alison, whom I've also known since college, stayed in the city when her children were little. Alison made city motherhood look like so much fun. Then again, she made everything look fun. That's one of the reasons that I loved to hang out with her when we were undergrads and housemates at Penn, and Upper West Side neighbors in New York before we had husbands and kids. Alison was always up for whatever you wanted to do—go to a party, see a movie, or go out for a drink. She showed up with her giant smile and dimpled chin, ready to have a good time. She was also always there when you needed her most, like right after Joey was born and my mom was dying. Alison arrived on my suburban doorstep, playing hooky from her job as an advertising executive in New York because, as she explained to me, she didn't think I sounded right over the phone. We spent the day together with baby Joey playing on the floor of my mother's bedroom as my mom rested after a particularly tough treatment. Alison kept my mother laughing as only she could. That was the last time Alison would ever see my mother.

Like so many other things in my life, my mother would not get to meet Alison's daughter, Isabel, who became close with my own daughter over the years. After Isabel was born, Alison hired nanny Gail, who was referred to her by a neighbor in her building. Much like Jane's nanny Lily, nanny Gail had her already established network of nannies from previous jobs. Gail was originally from Trinidad, like baby nurse Jackie, and lived in Brooklyn. She told Alison that she only took jobs on the Upper West Side because she could get there relatively easily from her home by subway. She also knew the West Side neighborhood well. That was just one of Gail's rules, and, luckily for her, she was in demand enough that she could put that rule and others into effect.

Alison appreciated how well Gail knew the neighborhood and kid-friendly spots. Nanny Gail told Alison and her husband Nathan about all these places, and they were most appreciative. Alison's kids got to know the doormen who worked in the buildings where they played during the weekdays with their nanny, her nanny friends, and the children they cared for. When Alison and Nathan strolled with their kids down West End Avenue on the weekends, some of the doormen waved to her children and knew them by name. Alison was amused. Her kids were known while she was a complete stranger—just the mother.

Lawyer Nina's kids in downtown Philadelphia also led a bit of a secretive life without their parents during the weekdays with their nanny Liza. Liza took Nina's kids out on the city bus to Reading Terminal Market to sample many Philadelphia delicacies. When Nina and Mark took the kids out to the market on the weekends, they were surprised to learn that many of the vendors knew their kids by name. The vendors also knew what foods the kids liked, including chicken cheesesteaks and shrimp dumplings, as they had those foods waiting. Nina and Mark were pleased to learn that their nanny was helping to expand their childrens' palates.

Rachel's Rules

The truth of the matter is that you live where you live, so when hiring a nanny, whether in the suburbs or the city, know the market and work within that market. If you live in the burbs, understand that you might not have as many qualified and professional nanny candidates to pull from. You may need to work a little harder to find a strong candidate that will stick with you over time. You should also know that you will not be paying top dollar in the suburbs like families do in the city.

If you live in the suburbs, it's just a fact of life that at some point your nanny will have to drive your kids around to where they need to be. You couldn't get by without this, so be prepared. Make sure your nanny has a car that you feel comfortable having your kids in, and supply her with the necessary car seats and with money for gas. Be clear on your rules for driving: no texting or talking on the phone (which you would hope she would already know, but don't take anything for granted). Make sure she knows how you feel—that your children are the most precious cargo to you and should be for her as well.

And if you live in the city, be ready to act fast to hire a good nanny candidate. Chances are, if you like a candidate, someone else probably does too, and they may hire her before you get the chance. Jane learned this the hard way. Also know that with the knowledge and experience of city nannies comes their own world that they will introduce your children to, and that you will only be introduced to that world to a certain extent. You must accept the fact that your children will have a social life that does not involve you. They will be exposed to new experiences and new people through their city caretakers. Use this experience and knowledge like Jane and Alison did to find out the best kid hangouts and the best music classes. Consider your city nanny to be another resource in this respect.

⤙ 4 ⤚

The Young and the Not So Young

I always wanted to find a clone of myself to be our nanny, but that wasn't very realistic. One of the many reasons I couldn't find a nanny clone is that nannies are generally either on the younger or older side of the mothers that want to employ them. I found that nanny candidates who were in their thirties like me had young children of their own. If they were going to work for me, they would have to bring their own small children along with them to my house while they watched my kids. That was an option that I did not want to explore in any way, shape, or form.

The Young Nannies

I was drawn to the young nannies. I wanted someone with lots of energy who could keep up with my children, and I related to the younger nannies. I guess there was a part of me that still saw myself as a recent college graduate ready to take on the world. That vision was crushed rather suddenly one day when one of our young nannies recommended a restaurant to me because her mom liked it. That hurt. I always thought the young nannies thought of me as a part of their generation. Clearly I was wrong about that.

I was a bit taken aback by how young our first nanny Amy looked when I first met her. But I figured that I looked that young right after I had graduated from college. Amy had short, dark hair, bright blue eyes, and a face full of freckles. She actually reminded me of myself if I had been a few inches shorter, didn't highlight my hair, and was able to pull off that cute pixie haircut. She had plenty of energy to keep up with baby, and eventually toddler, Joey. Nanny Amy always got right down on the floor and played with him, and she took him on long walks and ran around with him on the playground. She was silly with him and in many ways related to him better than she did to us. It worked.

I knew what nanny Amy was capable of, and I also learned about her limitations. She needed a lot of direction, and that was fine because I was happy to give it to her. Nanny Amy asked a lot of questions, especially when there was a change-up in the routine (i.e. moving from baby food to solid foods or from two little naps to one big nap). I definitely felt like a nanny mentor of sorts to her. She sought my reassurance a lot. I knew that nanny Amy did not bring a ton of confidence to the position, but I felt like she got a lot of good on-the-job training. When she left after almost two years of working for us to take the "real job" with better pay and health benefits, I was surprised. Neil? Not so much. He very correctly figured that Amy was in a transitory stage of her life and that she wouldn't work for us forever.

"She's a kid," he said when I told him that she was leaving and expressed how disappointed I was. "What did you expect? That she would grow old with us?" he remarked with a smile. I guess there was a part of me that secretly did. Neil came to the understanding much sooner than I did that the young nannies would not last that long, but still he let me make most of the nanny hiring and management decisions. After all, I was the one who had the most interaction with our nannies on a day-to-day basis.

Nanny number two, Ellie, was just a couple years older than Amy. She had more confidence than Amy as she had already worked as a nanny for another family. She didn't need as much direction or reassurance from me, but she too had her limitations. Nanny Ellie made a lot of assumptions about what was appropriate to do with little Joey. She sometimes took him out to lunch and met up with her friends. This was fine with me on occasion, but when she started regularly asking me for extra money for these lunch outings, I had to explain to her that I had bought lots of good food for Joey and for her to have in the house. She didn't need to be taking Joey out all around town to socialize with her friends.

Nanny Ellie got the message, but I honestly don't think she ever saw anything wrong with her lunch outings. I would never assume that it was okay to go out to lunch with friends while I was working and still get paid for that time. Since I was working part-time for the marketing company, I was paid as an independent consultant and billed all my hours. When I worked, I got paid, and when I didn't work, I didn't get paid. My job was pretty clear-cut. But nanny Ellie's job? Not so much.

When nanny Ellie left us after only four months to take the teaching job at the very last minute, I hired another young nanny. I could tell some of my friends were starting to doubt my judgment. This time would be different, I promised myself. And it was. While nanny number three, Molly, was in her early twenties just like Amy and Ellie, she seemed so much more mature. Molly had a very strong work ethic, and she had taken care of younger siblings and cousins. She had even worked for another family as a nanny in her late teenage years. I couldn't imagine working as a nanny at such a young age, but I could see that nanny Molly could have done it. She was an old soul.

I felt like we had the best of both worlds with her—the energy of a young nanny and the responsible nature of an older one. To this day, Neil still goes on record saying that Molly was his favorite nanny. I think that was in large part due to how neat she kept our house and how well she folded Joey and Rebecca's laundry. We had never seen anything like it. Nanny Molly showed me up in the housekeeping department, but it was more than that. Molly was strict with Joey while still maintaining a gentle and caring way with him.

Nanny Molly was with us through that tough transition from a family of three to a family of four. She worked for us throughout my pregnancy and then my maternity leave home with baby number two, Rebecca. Molly was a great source of peace and calmness at home amidst the craziness of life with a newborn and a toddler. The only problem was when she became unexpectedly pregnant and had to leave. I was more shocked by the pregnancy than I think even she was, and she was really caught off guard. That was the risk we took with hiring another young nanny.

Young Julie, nanny number four, was a quick hire and knee-jerk reaction to needing someone, anyone, after losing Molly to the surprise pregnancy. Nanny Julie was a regression back to someone who seemed even younger than nanny Amy, but I liked her during the interview. Again I was drawn to the young nannies. I guess I had a type. I sort of knew early on that hiring Julie was a mistake. She needed way too much direction, and I think she viewed me as an older sister or perhaps even mother figure. She constantly told me stories about her boyfriend and the ins and outs of her personal life. She was never professional enough.

My lawyer friend Nina saw a big difference in the young nanny she hired after she and her family moved out to the suburbs from Philadelphia. Her second nanny Debby was way younger than her older and more experienced first nanny Liza. Nina thought nanny Debby would be a good change for the family as her kids were getting older and only needed after-school care. Nina thought young nanny Debby would be more fun for her kids, and that she would be great to drive them around to all of their sports and play fun games with them. Nanny Debby did all of that. Nina sometimes came home from work to hear the kids laughing while they played board games in the basement with nanny Debby. And Debby was able to take one kid to the soccer field and play on the playground with the other two during the soccer practice.

While nanny Debby could multitask and had plenty of energy to keep up with Nina's kids, she got easily distracted. There were also times when Nina came home from work to find the kids finishing up their homework at the kitchen table while nanny Debby texted with her friends. Sometimes nanny Debby couldn't complete a full sentence on a report from the day without her phone beeping several times with texting updates. She was never quite fully there giving her undivided attention to Nina's kids.

My friend Stacey's young nanny, Gina (the same nanny who got the DUI), was in college part-time while she worked for the family, and Stacey thought she had a great set-up. She assumed that nanny Gina could help the kids with their homework in the afternoon, as Gina was a student and should be in a similar mindset. That wasn't the case. Once the kids got past third grade, nanny Gina was not so great with homework help. She didn't understand the "new math," and she was never able to figure it out. Luckily for Stacey, her oldest son, who was in sixth grade, could help the younger boys with their work, and then he waited until Stacey was home and Phil finished up his work so that they could help him. It wasn't ideal and perhaps an older and more experienced nanny would have been a bigger help in the homework department, but like so many other nanny situations, Gina worked for them.

My friend Suzanne the social worker was also attracted to the young nannies for many of the same reasons that I was. When the young nanny candidates got down on the floor and played with her kids or ran around with them in the backyard, that was it. Suzanne fell in love. That didn't mean that she always stayed in love. She recognized the limitations in some of her younger nannies, but she was able to work through many of them. Suzanne understood that she had to give young nanny Rori exact and very explicit instructions on everything. She could take nothing for granted.

Suzanne was initially annoyed when she would come home from work to a kitchen sink piled high with dirty dishes. That issue got resolved after Suzanne explained to nanny Rori that she should rinse all the dishes and put them in the dishwasher and sponge off the kitchen table too. Suzanne still has step-by-step instructions taped to the side of her refrigerator on how to work their toaster oven. She initially wrote them out for Rori, and some of her subsequent young nannies have used them too.

The Hot Nannies

Many working mothers I know will not hire a nanny if she is too good looking.

"It's just not worth it," one mother and doctor who employed several wonderful au pairs said to me. "I know that my husband loves me very much and is extremely faithful, but there are nights when I'm on call and sleeping at the hospital, and he just doesn't need to be home with a gorgeous young woman living in our house who lovingly cares for our kids every day."

She had a point. So whenever the family interviewed candidates through the au pair agency, they made sure to chat with her via FaceTime or Skype, or at the very least to see a picture of her. It is often the case when hiring an au pair that the family does not get to meet the candidate until she already has the job and comes to the United States to work. The "not too beautiful" factor was simply another box to check off under a big list of requirements for this family. It was right up there with nonsmoker and ability to drive.

Neil and I never had that problem. We did hire one really gorgeous young woman named Danielle to help care for our children on a family beach vacation. Neil and I were equally smitten with her perfect looks and joked to each other about them. As beautiful as she was, her caretaking skills with the kids were even more impressive. One day she took little Rebecca for a walk on the beach and came back with a butterfly that she managed to capture in her own hands. Rebecca and Danielle played with the butterfly for a while, and then Danielle set the butterfly free, having taught Rebecca a whole impromptu lesson on the lifecycle of caterpillar to butterfly. It was unbelievable.

I never worried even for a minute that anything could happen between Neil and Danielle. I knew even more so than my doctor friend that Neil would never ever cheat on me, and I also knew that Danielle viewed Neil as an old man, even though he was only in his mid-thirties at the time. As Danielle giggled at one of Neil's jokes in the kitchen one evening, she remarked how Neil reminded her of her dad. That was a wakeup call for Neil. He was invisible to her. We joked about her comment later that night in the privacy of our own bedroom.

Lawyer Nina and her husband Mark also had a very solid marriage, and Nina had no worries about her super texting and also super good-looking young nanny, Debby. Nina took it all in stride when Debby took a week off from work to get breast augmentation surgery as she very bluntly explained to Nina via text message. Nina found the need for such elective surgery a bit ridiculous and also wondered why Debby was so open with her on that front.

"I would have lied," Nina told me. "I just would have said that I was going away on vacation and needed the time off. But hey, at least she felt comfortable enough with me to be so honest." Mark was also intrigued with the openness on the breast augmentation surgery front, and they laughed together about the absurdity of the whole situation.

Stacey's second nanny, Serena, was a beautiful young woman when she started working for the family, and even though her husband Phil worked at home all day while nanny Serena was in the house, Stacey had no problem with the situation. Especially because, as Stacey explained, over time Serena's looks started to fade as she put on a lot of weight because of all the food that she ate while in Stacey's house.

The Not-So-Young Nannies

It took me a long time, but I did learn my lesson after hiring, employing, and then losing four young nannies. While each young nanny had her own strengths and unique qualities, the common factor in every case was that each young nanny was in a very transitional stage of her life. Not one of them worked for us as long as I had hoped they would—for better or for worse. I made a very purposeful decision when looking for nanny number five to find someone who was a bit more established in her life. Someone who knew what she wanted to be when she grew up because she was already grown up. I finally knew that we needed a professional nanny . . . a real nanny . . . a career nanny. And for us this meant an older nanny. Nanny number five: Alice.

When we first met Alice she had all the right answers to our questions. And even though I had experienced the revolving door of too many young nannies, I still wondered if Alice would have the energy to keep up with our kids. She was in her mid-fifties, which was significantly older than the other women I had hired in the past, and she was also a large woman. I didn't want to discriminate on age or size, but the thought did occur to me and to Neil. The reference from her last family was so filled with accolades though, so we hired her. I was determined to make the nanny Alice situation work and to stick. I even took a couple of days to work from home in the beginning so that I could observe Alice in her work and provide some on-the-job training if necessary.

It wasn't. I was so impressed with Alice and all that I saw as I worked from home (i.e. spied on her and the kids). The house was quieter (in a really good way) than it had ever been when any other nanny had been in charge. Nanny Alice sat down on the floor next to baby Rebecca on her play mat and watched her try to move around, encouraging her to push herself up on her hands and get ready to crawl. Alice worked with Joey on art projects and talked to him about his budding interest in sports.

Nanny Alice had about a thousand times more confidence and more experience than did the younger nannies. She was so sure of herself that she rarely asked me any questions in the mornings or evenings, and almost never called me at work with a question or a problem. Alice really was the professional nanny that I had always wanted, and she prided herself on that. She took full credit for getting Rebecca to crawl and for potty training her. I was happy to give it to her, but I do believe that we had some part in it, and of course a lot of the credit goes to Rebecca. I'm pretty sure that Rebecca would not have gone off to college still immobile or in diapers with or without training from nanny Alice.

While Alice was the oldest nanny we ever employed, in some ways, she was still very young at heart. She kept up on many of the latest little kid fads and news from her grandchildren, and she loved to take the kids to play out in the backyard on the swing set. However, she did get sick . . . a lot. Nanny Alice was a diabetic and she was up-front about it during her interview, but she assured us that her health would not be a factor in her work. It was.

The first full winter that Alice worked for us, she called out sick too many times to count. It was tough, as I had to scramble for backup sitters so that I could get to work. But there was nothing I could do about it. I didn't want her around my kids when she was sick, and I felt bad for her that she got sick so easily. Nanny Alice often developed bronchitis, or laryngitis, or, as she would say to me on the phone some mornings just as I was getting ready to go to work, she just "wasn't feeling well." I couldn't make her come to work. We got by.

Social worker Suzanne employed an older nanny named Candice. Candice was a retired nurse in her sixites, and she brought lots of years of experience to the job. Suzanne liked that Candice brought sock puppets to the interview to play with the kids, and she often brought art supplies to draw with Suzanne's daughter. Suzanne noticed a big difference in Candice versus her younger nannies. Nanny Candice was in complete control when she was working, and she didn't ask for or need any direction. Suzanne didn't even have to think about remembering to pay nanny Candice. Before Suzanne took out her checkbook at the end of the week, Candice presented Suzanne with an invoice complete with her work hours and job responsibilities for that time period. Although Suzanne found this routine a bit odd, she liked that Candice took charge. It was one less thing for Suzanne to think about.

Suzanne was a little concerned with nanny Candice carrying her baby son Ryan up and down the stairs in her house. Although Candice played very nicely with the kids, she was a bit frail, and Suzanne sometimes imagined her collapsing and tumbling down the steps with Ryan in her arms. While this nightmare never came to fruition,

Candice did eventually give up her position because of a broken arm and other health-related problems. Suzanne was sad to see Candice leave, but she was somewhat relieved. She always figured ailing health would take Candice away from them.

The Old-School Old Nanny

When I was a small child in the 1970s, my parents employed an older nanny named Mrs. Dougherty to care for my brother and me. We always called her Mrs. Dougherty. I don't think I ever knew her first name. Mrs. Dougherty's exact age was also unknown, but we figured she was old . . . very old. Mrs. Dougherty was a tall woman with soft white curly hair and even softer wrinkly skin. I remember her wearing flowered blouses with her own hand-knit cardigan sweaters, khaki polyester pants, and her oversized cat-eyed glasses. She was a widow with grown children and grandchildren, and she loved to take care of kids.

My parents hired Mrs. Dougherty to watch my brother and me from the time we were babies (at just fourteen months apart) until we were about ten and eleven years old. My mother didn't take her two babies out of the house that much.

"In those days, there weren't five thousand classes and activities for kids like there are now," my mother used to say. Mrs. Dougherty watched us when my mother went grocery shopping, ran errands, and volunteered at the nursing home where she was very involved. In those days, my father traveled a lot for work, and when my mother traveled with him, Mrs. Dougherty stayed with my brother and me at our house overnight. She also watched us on Saturday nights when my parents always went out to an adults-only dinner.

The Mrs. Dougherty sleepovers were the best. Mrs. Dougherty was so old that she had false teeth, and she didn't put her teeth back in for breakfast. My brother and I loved to watch her gum her way through the meal. That provided a whole morning of amusement. Unlike my parents, Mrs. Dougherty did take us out of the house . . . in the backseat of her mustard-colored Chevy Cavalier without car seats or even seat belts. We sat on top of newspapers because Mrs. Dougherty didn't want us to get the seats dirty. She took us to church services on the occasional Sunday morning. Did I mention that we are Jewish? She also took us to bingo night to play in her game at the American Legion. We became pretty good young bingo players.

My brother and I thought Mrs. Dougherty was a great cook. In the elementary school days, we were excited to get off the school bus and find the Cavalier in the driveway.

"Looks like a Mrs. Dougherty Manwich night," my brother would say to me with a smile. Mrs. Dougherty introduced us to Manwich, Chef Boyardee, and SpaghettiOs, and her grilled cheese with hot chocolate was one of my most favorite meals of all time. Mrs. Dougherty also knit winter hats, gloves, and sweaters for us. I wore the pink pom-pom hat with the strings extended down the flappy ears until I outgrew it, even though it was very itchy.

I really have all good memories of Mrs. Dougherty, and so does my brother. My mother never had anything bad to say about her. After I lost my mother to cancer and struggled to take care of my young kids while working, I'd sometimes ask my father how our mother had managed back in the day. His response was always something like: "I don't know. She had Mrs. Dougherty."

Mrs. Dougherty really did seem like the answer to all of our prayers. Who knows? Maybe our memories are clouded, and maybe my mother would tell me differently now if she could, but I kind of doubt it. I think things were different then . . . much easier and definitely much simpler. I have to admit that I am a little jealous of that time.

I'm not sure, though, how employable an older lady like Mrs. Dougherty would be today. I don't see 21st century parents approving of some of the things she did with us (i.e. taking Jewish kids to church services and then feeding them way over-processed dinners and gumming it up at the breakfast table). But then again, who am I to judge? My parents had no problem with these activities, and I think they were pretty good parents. Plus, we turned out fine . . . at least good enough to know not to allow those types of things to occur in our own grown-up houses.

Rachel's Rules

THE YOUNG AND THE NOT-SO-YOUNG NANNIES

You should know that you will never replicate yourself, so don't try to. You will generally end up hiring a nanny who is younger or older than you. That's simply how the demographics play out. Know that, but also remember to measure each candidate on her own merits and qualifications. You might assume that a young nanny has more energy than an older one, and then find out otherwise. The same goes for assuming that an older nanny does not have enough energy. Take each candidate on a case-by-case basis.

Also consider the age and stages of life that your children are in. Some older nannies are better for young babies who are relatively immobile and don't require a lot of running around. Older nannies also usually have more experience and qualifications. Many parents will find this especially attractive when looking for someone to care for a newborn. Older nannies seem to be more committed to working for one family for the longer term. They are more settled in their lives and not looking forward to moving on to the next phase, whatever that may be. They are also more sure of themselves in their positions, and do not need nearly as much direction as their younger counterparts.

One very important lesson I learned from my days of employing younger nannies is that you can't expect them to stick around forever. That's just not realistic. Our young nannies always left for one reason or another. Understand that your young nanny will be moving on at some point, and it will most often be sooner rather than later. Also expect to offer direction and on-the-job training to young nannies. Because they don't have a lot of experience, they will need this. If you think you are up for being a nanny mentor of sorts, then go for it. But if not, stick to an older and more experienced nanny.

As my kids got older, I was drawn even more to younger nannies because my kids loved them and had fun with them. Nannies number six and seven, Madeline and April, who were actually after-school sitters, played lots of fun games with my kids, and they knew about the latest television shows and pop stars that my kids followed. Be careful though, and set boundaries with younger nannies. If you don't, you may end up taking care of them too much.

☞ 5 ☜

We Are Family . . . or Are We?

My whole family is close. Really close. I still talk to my father and brother almost every day, and also to my aunt, my late mother's sister. When I was growing up, my grandparents were over at our house all the time, and my father has been known to pop by my grown-up house for a quick visit with our kids or a weeknight family dinner. My grown-up nuclear family of four is equally as close as my original one. There are no secrets among us, and we are always there for each other no matter what.

Over our years of employing many nannies, we've developed close relationships with a few of them. Some more than others. I tried to keep each relationship as professional as I could, but that was easier said than done. Even though a nanny is technically an employee, she is given the task of caring for the people most precious to you: your children. She sees you at your most vulnerable times, and she becomes a part of your most intimate family relationships. A nanny may see you breastfeed your baby, she'll change your childrens' diapers, and she'll care for your sick children when you need her most so that you can go to work. Somewhere along the way, a nanny can and will start to feel like family. The lines become blurred for better or for worse.

Blurred Lines

My friend Suzanne the social worker always had trouble with those blurred lines. She invited each of her nannies to her childrens' birthday parties because she thought that was the right thing to do, but she always felt funny about it. Suzanne didn't want her nannies to feel obligated to attend the family parties. After all, each nanny spent plenty of time with her children during the work week. She also didn't want them to feel obligated to buy her kids presents, or have to play with them during what should have been their off-duty hours. Suzanne sometimes wondered if she should pay the nanny for the time she spent at the birthday party, but she thought that might offend her too. It was a slippery slope. And so every January and every August, without fail Suzanne invited her nanny to her childrens' birthday parties. Suzanne often found that the nanny accepted the invitation, but usually canceled at the last minute. That was fine with her. Suzanne knew she was doing the right thing by sending the invitation. She understood that the nanny felt obligated to accept and then understood when the nanny ultimately decided not to attend the party.

While Suzanne often felt like an older sister or mother figure to her nanny Rori, it was nanny Rori who in many ways brought Suzanne's baby son Ryan into her own family as a surrogate son or little brother. Suzanne's older daughter Charlotte was in school for a big chunk of the day while Rori cared for little Ryan. Rori often brought Ryan back to her parents' house where she still lived. In the summer, Rori took Ryan swimming in their family pool, and around the holidays, Rori and her mother took Ryan to meet Santa Claus at the mall, and even had a stocking for Ryan hung on their mantle. Suzanne was happy that Rori felt so close to her son, and much like city moms Jane, Alison, and Nina, Suzanne was amused by Ryan's secret life with his "other family," as she called them.

Stacey's third nanny Mariella became very close to the family. When nanny Mariella gave birth to her first child while still working for Stacey and Phil, it was Phil who drove Mariella and her new baby boy home from the hospital. Mariella's fiancé could not take the day off from work at his new job in construction, and since Phil worked from home, he was available. Stacey and Mariella had worked out a deal during the pregnancy by which Mariella would take a couple months maternity leave, and would then return to work with her baby. On the day that Mariella went into labor early, Stacey scrambled to find a backup sitter so that her husband could pick up her nanny and nanny's new baby from the hospital. Stacey recognized the unusual situation they were in, but they loved nanny Mariella. She felt a bit like family, and as Stacey explained, "That's what you do for family."

Our fourth nanny, Julie, felt very comfortable around us. She was also very close to her family, and by extension, we got to know that family and inner circle fairly well. Julie's boyfriend Nick sometimes came along with her when she watched our kids on a Saturday night. Nick was great with Joey, and we didn't mind that he was there. Julie told me all about her aunt, her mother's sister who was diagnosed with cancer a few months into her working for us. Julie was about the age I was when my own mother was diagnosed with cancer, so I think she looked to me for advice. I was generally happy to offer it as best as I could, but I was also pretty pressed for time in my comings and goings before and after work. My main concern was making sure nanny Julie was taking good care of my kids.

One Friday in the early afternoon Julie called me at my office in tears. Her aunt had taken a turn for the worse, and she really wanted, actually needed, as she told me, to go see her that afternoon. I was about to walk into a meeting at work, and I really couldn't leave. I tried to be as understanding as possible, and Neil happened to be working at a client location that was pretty close to our house. I knew he didn't have that many pressing meetings, and so I called him and asked him to go home to relieve Julie because of her sick aunt.

Neil was definitely hesitant to leave work, especially since he recognized better than I did that Julie was our employee. She was responsible for caring for our kids for the agreed upon hours so that we could go to work and do our jobs. But he also knew that I was in a bind. I was almost always the one who came home when there was a childcare issue. That was our understood arrangement, and it made sense and usually worked for us. Neil made more money than I did, his office was much further away from home than mine was, he traveled a lot, and he had little flexibility. But it was his turn that day, so he went home and took over for weepy Julie. Neil later told me how awkward it was for him when he got back to our house, as he wasn't really sure how to console her. He was not thrilled about having to do this. I understood where he was coming from, but I didn't really have a choice.

I know that a tougher boss may have told her nanny that she had to stay at work for the rest of the day, but I felt bad for nanny Julie. She felt like more than just an employee. Nanny Julie's aunt recovered from that tough day and hung in there a lot longer than anyone had expected. I tried to limit the personal talk as much as I could during the mornings and evenings, but that wasn't so easy with Julie. I was also partially to blame. I always wanted her to feel comfortable around us. Perhaps she became too comfortable.

We got to know nanny number five, Alice's family, probably more than we wanted to. Alice had lots of grandchildren who lived nearby, and two of them were about the same age as Joey and Rebecca. Alice told me one day that she had taken my kids out to meet the grandchildren and her daughter for lunch. This was during the break between school and camp for Joey. I thought that was nice in that the kids got to meet and play with some new kids, but I didn't want her to make a habit out of it.

As Neil said to me, "Alice should be focused on our kids when we are paying her to watch them, and not just hanging out with her grandchildren." I knew he was right, but like so many other working mothers, I didn't want to upset our nanny. Alice was finally the real nanny that I had wanted, and she and her daughter and grandchildren got to be pretty close to our kids. So what if she hung out a bit with them on the job?

We were all invited to Alice's grandson's birthday party at a nearby park. I took the kids to the party as Neil had work to catch up on that Saturday afternoon. I also knew he thought it was kind of ridiculous that I was going to our nanny's grandson's birthday party. I thought it was the nice thing to do and would be fun for the kids. It was . . . sort of. I got to meet all of Alice's family including her husband, all her children, all the grandchildren, her sister, brother-in-law, and nieces and nephews. They were all so nice to me, but I did feel a bit awkward. Joey, Rebecca, and I were the only non-relatives at the party.

Nanny Alice didn't feel awkward at all. She considered us to be a part of her extended family. We came from very different backgrounds, but we were connected through the children. Alice and her family were very faithful Christians, and she spoke fairly often of Jesus Christ and his wondrous healing powers. This made me a bit uncomfortable since I didn't believe in his existence as the son of God (even though Jesus was Jewish, I reminded myself and Neil). When I developed a pretty bad stomach infection one summer, Alice prayed for me and insisted that her prayers helped me get better. I believed it was more the very strong antibiotics prescribed to me by a top-notch gastroenterologist, but who knows? Maybe nanny Alice's prayers helped just a little?

When we bought new patio furniture, I gave our old wicker furniture to nanny Alice, and she was happy to take it. The same went for old pots and pans and some other items from our house. I was thrilled to give them to her. It did strike me as funny though, when I went to her house for the first time and noticed that it looked like a mini version of our house with all of the hand-me-downs. I took it as a compliment. Nanny Alice liked our taste.

Alice started to feel somewhat like family to me, albeit a very different type of family. When she told me one day after I came home from work that she had been diagnosed with cancer, I was very concerned and sad for her and her family. Nanny Alice had it all under control, though. She said that her prognosis was good and that she would get through it with flying colors. I admired her positive attitude. It reminded me of my mother's attitude, which I believe helped to extend the quality and length of her life when she was undergoing her treatment for cancer. Nanny Alice quickly put a plan in place for the month she had to take off from work because of her treatments. She had arranged for her sister to fill in for her so that my work schedule would not be interrupted. I so appreciated that. She went out of her way for us—like any good family member would do.

Personal Space

Although nannies do become a part of the very intimate space in your household, there are instances when you need to put some boundaries on that space. Sonny, an Information Technology specialist and mother to three boys, one of whom goes to school with my son, needed to find that space with her nanny, Colleen—the hugging nanny. Every night before nanny Colleen left the house, she insisted on giving and getting a hug in return from the boys. At first Sonny thought the hugging was an adorable exchange of affection between her nanny and her children, but when the hugs became extended to Sonny, she felt uncomfortable. Sonny never hugged her boss in her office before she went home, but she didn't want to upset Colleen. So she hugged her back . . . every night.

Sonny's husband Alan wanted no part of the hugging. When he was home in time to see nanny Colleen, and to see the hug coming, he walked as fast as he could upstairs into his bedroom so he couldn't get or give the hug. Alan established a rule that nanny Colleen was not allowed in the master bedroom. The rule seemed a bit harsh to Sonny at first, but once the hugging became an every night occurrence, she wished she too could quickly escape into the nanny-free hug zone—the master bedroom.

Lori, my friend the accountant and mom to two young girls, also struggled with boundaries for her long-time live-in nanny, Tricia. Nanny Tricia, much like the hugging nanny Colleen, had developed her own nightly ritual. Before heading downstairs to her room in the basement for the night, Tricia would tell each of Lori's daughters that she loved them. And like Sonny initially did with hugging nanny Colleen, Lori thought this was a nice display of affection, but over time it got to be a bit much. Nanny Tricia would not go downstairs until she heard an "I love you too" from each girl. It was sometimes hard to drag the words out of the kids. The girls were usually focused on playing with their toys, watching television, or catching up with their mother who they hadn't seen all day. After a while, Lori had to very carefully explain to Tricia that she wouldn't always get the "I love yous" out of the kids on demand. After all, Lori didn't, and she was their mother.

An old high school friend of mine, Courtney, who worked as a learning specialist in New York City, didn't have an overly hugging or lovey nanny, but she did have one that had no concept of personal space or boundaries. This became apparent to Courtney after her nanny Joanne came into Courtney's bathroom and sat down on the closed toilet seat and started talking to Courtney about her personal life. Courtney was trying to blow dry her hair and put on a little makeup so that she could look halfway decent for work. That was no small feat for Courtney with two rambunctious boys under the age of three, and it became even harder with nanny Joanne chatting away just a couple feet away from her in the bathroom. Courtney couldn't imagine even her closest friends and family members sitting on the toilet seat right by her. They understood boundaries and the concept of personal space. Nanny Joanne clearly did not.

My neighbor and good friend Diane, a speech pathologist and mother to three children, employed nanny Jeannie for five years. Over the years, Jeannie grew very close to Diane and her family, but it took time. I got that, as it was initially difficult for me to get close to Diane when both of our families moved into the same neighborhood years ago. Diane seemed shy and even guarded to me at first—the complete opposite of the way I was. I think she was shocked when I showed up at her doorstep on the day they moved into the neighborhood with a plate of homemade brownies and little Rebecca who was ready to play with her kids. It took several play and lunch dates initiated by me to get to know Diane, and once I did, she let her guard down and really opened up. She has an unbelievable dry sense of humor and makes me laugh so hard about anything and everything. She is so laid back, and is just fun to be with. In fact, she reminds me of the female version of Neil, and she is a foodie just like him. Whenever Neil and I go out to dinner with Diane and her husband, Justin, Neil and Diane pick the restaurant. Justin and I just show up, and we all have a good time together.

Diane and Justin almost always have good stories to tell at these dinners. Like how their nanny Jeannie felt so comfortable with them that she brought her own dirty laundry over to their house and washed it in their laundry room. Diane explained to me how she never told nanny Jeannie that this was acceptable, but she also never told her that it was unacceptable. It was just something that she did. The two women never spoke about it until Justin found out. He was less than thrilled when he walked into the laundry room to get one of his shirts before work and found nanny Jeannie's bras hanging right in front of him on the drying rack. Justin told Jeannie that she couldn't do her own wash at their house. Diane stayed out of it.

The Ties that Bind

When a nanny starts to feel like family and not so much an employee, the employer begins to treat the nanny as such. This happened to Michelle, a marketing research professional and mom to two children who had recently moved from Atlanta to the Philadelphia suburbs when I met her through our children. Our daughters played sports together, and Michelle was looking to network to find a new job in Philly. I knew that she wouldn't have a problem finding work as she seemed so bright and friendly. She could talk even more than I could, and she was very engaging. Michelle was very open with me about her experience as a working mom and her struggles with her nanny back in Atlanta.

Michelle and her husband Ed had employed nanny Nora for two years, and they took good care of her. Nanny Nora had a lot of financial troubles over the years. She found herself without a car, and because she needed to get to and from Michelle and Ed's house and drive their children to and from school, Michelle and Ed bought her a used car—a Ford Explorer. It wasn't just a car to use while she was driving their kids. It was her car to use whenever. Nanny Nora kept the car at her house and used it on her own during the evenings and weekends.

Nanny Nora so appreciated Michelle and Ed's generosity, and she was thrilled to finally have a good car of her own. One Saturday afternoon while driving around without the kids, nanny Nora totaled the car, and she didn't have insurance on it to get it repaired. Michelle and Ed were in a bind. They loved nanny Nora, and she was so good with their kids, but they were upset about the accident. They were also upset with Nora because she never got insurance on the car, which she told them she would do. They felt like nanny Nora was their older child who had lied to them. They still loved her, and they really needed her. So Michelle and Ed bought Nora another car. This time it was a used, dark purple minivan affectionately called "the purple hippo" by the kids.

The purple hippo held up for a while, and nanny Nora took the kids wherever they needed to go in it. But again, one weekend afternoon, there was an incident. Nanny Nora was pulled over by a police officer for speeding. The officer discovered that Nora's license had been revoked because she failed to appear in court after the old Ford Explorer had been totaled in the accident. Michelle and Ed knew nothing about this. They were shocked to receive a call from Nora's sister telling them that Nora was being held in Atlanta County jail for driving with a revoked license and failure to appear in court. Nora had asked her sister to call Michelle and Ed as she needed money to post bail.

Again, Michelle and Ed felt they were stuck. They understood that they would not have let a situation go this far with an employee at one of their offices, but Nora was more than just an employee. She lovingly cared for their kids, and although she was far from perfect, the kids loved her. Michelle and Ed knew that Nora was a really good person who happened to make a lot of bad decisions. They contributed some money (along with Nora's sister) to bail nanny Nora out of jail, and Nora came back to work for the family.

My good friend from college and working New York City mom, Alison, had a work colleague who became very involved in her nanny's personal life. Alison's colleague ended up paying her nanny's hospital bills when the nanny underwent chemotherapy treatment to fight breast cancer, as the nanny did not have health insurance. Alison's colleague loved her nanny. She felt like family to her and to her kids, and she would do whatever it took to help her on her road to recovery.

Leigh, a teacher and mom to two children, who lives just north of New York City, employs nanny Daisy, who feels much like family to her. Nanny Daisy sort of feels like family to us as my family is so close to Leigh's. Leigh's husband Fred grew up with Neil, and I went to college with Leigh and Fred. They claim to have set us up at a party in New York City almost two decades ago, but we think they may just be taking the credit after we hit it off that night. Whatever the case may be, I am forever grateful to have them in our lives. We go away with Leigh and Fred and their children Bradley and Daphne every year. They are one of, if not the only family, that we can vacation with as we all get along so well. Neil knows when I'm on the phone with Leigh, as he hears us talking about family, friendship, and complicated relationships, then very seamlessly changing gears to review the latest trends in fall jackets and super-high boots. I felt like I had known Leigh my whole life when I met her on the front porch of a sorority house during our freshman year in college. There was an instant connection, and it has never gone away.

Leigh and I both hold a lot of value in our close-knit families, both the families we grew up with and the families we created with our husbands, our children, and our friendships. Unfortunately for us, we both learned at a fairly young age what real pain and loss feel like. I think that's why we can have deep talks, and then on a whim lighten it up. I so get her and she gets me. We always say that we wish we lived closer so that we could hang out all the time, and I've told her on occasion that I'm even a bit jealous of her nanny Daisy who does get to hang out with her family way more than I can. Leigh was lucky to have found Daisy six years ago based on a recommendation from an old babysitter, and Daisy too was lucky to have found Leigh and her family. They have the closest nanny/family relationship that I have ever seen. Leigh's son Bradley drew a picture of his family for a kindergarten class project and included a stick figure of nanny Daisy right in between the stick figure of himself and his mom. The picture still hangs on the family's refrigerator door now, years later.

Leigh also became very close to her baby nurse, Georgia. Georgia helped Leigh to care for her daughter Daphne after a very difficult pregnancy. Georgia stayed with the family for several months, and in between late night feedings and swaddling lessons, Leigh and Georgia had endless conversations. Leigh loved to talk with Georgia, much like I did with our baby nurse Jackie. Leigh and Georgia kept in close touch over the years, and one day Georgia asked Leigh and Fred to be the godparents to her first granddaughter. They were touched by the gesture, and so was Georgia when they took on the role with enthusiasm and attended her granddaughter's christening.

Our after-school sitter Madeline, who we found through the babysitting club at the gym, wanted our kids to play a role in a big milestone in her life. One summer afternoon on our way to the beach, I received the following text from Madeline: "Soooooooooo I may be getting married on November 5th . . . Would Joey and Rebecca like to be my ring bearer and flower girl?:)))"

I wasn't sure what to make of the message. I was really happy for Madeline, but I didn't know that she was so serious with her boyfriend, and I also didn't know that she felt close enough to us to offer our children such roles of honor in her own wedding. I guess Madeline thought of us as family, and the more I thought about it, the more I realized that we had similar feelings too. I mean Madeline sometimes refers to me as her "other mother," and I often hug her hello when she comes over to watch the kids when I haven't seen her for a couple weeks. I guess we are some kind of family.

Rachel's Rules

WE ARE FAMILY . . . OR ARE WE?

Understand up front that when you employ someone to care for your children in your home on a regular basis, they will develop relationships with your kids, and oftentimes with you and your spouse, that are something more than just the typical employee/employer relationships. It's almost impossible for those bonds not to form, and that is usually fine. It would even be a little strange if those relationships didn't grow into something more.

Be careful though. Things could go too far, as in the case of Michelle and Ed, when they felt like they were financing nanny Nora above and beyond what should have been their responsibilities. Know your limits. Establish boundaries and put them into place. Otherwise your nanny may join you every morning in the bathroom while you are trying to get ready for work, like my high school friend Courtney's nanny did.

I've always had a tough time with boundaries. The lines between my nanny and my family usually became blurred. I told myself that I'd take each situation on a case-by-case basis, but then as Neil often pointed out, I gave in to the nanny as if she were a member of my family. I understood this, and I was fine with it. Perhaps some nannies would not have gotten as close to me or my children if I didn't do this and put out that warm and friendly (sometimes too warm and friendly) vibe.

$\backsim 6 \backsim$

You Are Not the Boss of Me

When I worked for the large magazine company in New York, I always knew where I stood with my bosses, and I'm pretty sure that my direct reports knew where they stood with me. Things were laid out very clearly, and there was a direct chain of reports from the most junior position to the most senior one. We had a whole human resources department dedicated to making sure this was the case. This is often not the case for nannies and the families who employ them. In fact, it sometimes becomes unclear as to who is the nanny and who is the boss.

Someone Has to Be Tough

If it had not been for our third nanny, Molly, Joey might still be soothing himself to sleep with a pacifier today as an eleven-year-old fifth grader. Molly was the one who told me it was time to get rid of the pacifier, even though Joey only used it in the crib for his afternoon nap and at night right before he went to sleep. I knew she was right, and I let her take charge of the pacifier situation. Nanny Molly managed to get through two days of Joey napping without the pacifier. I had to stay strong at night and just let him "cry it out," as per Molly's instructions.

On that second night, however, I couldn't take the crying and running up and down the steps as I was then six months into my second pregnancy. So I caved and gave Joey the one lonely pacifier that I found buried in a pile of his stuffed animals in the corner of his crib. As nanny Molly got Joey dressed the next morning while I tried to sneak out the door for work without getting busted, I heard a "Rachel" from upstairs. I knew I was in trouble. Nanny Molly found the contraband pacifier in the crib, and I had ruined her two days of hard work. Like a child whose hand had been caught in the cookie jar, I confessed.

Even though I was the employer and nanny Molly the employee, she was clearly the boss in many situations. That was fine by me. I needed someone to take more control at home, and Molly liked being that person. I was stressed at work as I was getting ready to take a maternity leave, and I was also worried about how Joey would adapt to life with a new baby sibling. Nanny Molly made that time much easier for me. I knew Joey was testing me as he knew big changes were coming as my belly grew. Nanny Molly was firm with Joey, but she still had a fun-loving and playful way with him. She also ran our house like no one else. I sometimes look at our house today and wonder how organized it would be if nanny Molly still worked for us or, rather, I worked for her. Nanny Molly was a good boss.

My good friend Kate from graduate school also employed a bossy nanny named Rita. Kate moved to California after getting her MBA in Michigan. And after working for a few companies, she went on to start her own home design business and later a home products start-up.

Kate and I were in the same section in business school, which meant that we took all of our classes together. We were not the typical MBA students in that we did not have the traditional finance, accounting, engineering, or economics backgrounds that many of our classmates did. We both came from creative sides of business and felt a little overwhelmed when our professors quickly reviewed balance sheets in accounting class and the Capital Asset Pricing Model in finance. Lucky for us, we befriended another student named Daryn who had a hardcore engineering background. Daryn taught us everything. We couldn't have gotten through business school without her. She was our boss, and a good one at that. Kate, like me, liked having a boss in most every situation. We liked having someone to tell us what to do, whether it was putting the credits to the left and the debits to the right on an accounting balance sheet, or getting a baby to sleep through the night.

And so much like I did with nanny Molly, Kate and her husband John hired bossy nanny Rita after their daughter Logan was born. Nanny Rita often interrupted Kate's workdays with phone calls or text messages wanting to know when she would be paid next. Although Kate had clearly laid out the details of the work relationship, including a pay day every other Friday, Rita still took it upon herself to take charge and insist on getting paid whenever she needed the money. Kate needed nanny Rita and didn't want to deal with the payment issue or with finding a new nanny. So Kate complied with the on-demand pay schedule, although she sort of felt like she was being extorted for the money.

Kate gave birth to Logan during a very busy time in her career. She was commuting between California and

New York while working with another design firm in New York. The hours and travel were crazy, especially since Kate had a new baby who she was still nursing. Kate was passionate about the business and suspected the New York firm would soon buy her own business. Eventually they did. Kate knew that she wouldn't be commuting like that forever, but she had to do it for at least a few months. Kate was determined to make the bicoastal situation work, and she needed nanny Rita to help her do that. So nanny Rita traveled with Kate and baby Logan from California to New York and back every week.

When Kate was at work in New York, nanny Rita watched Logan using their hotel as home base, and when they were in California, Rita adjusted to life as the West Coast nanny back at their house. In many ways, Kate was more dependent on Rita than Rita was on Kate. Kate felt like she was working for the company in New York and for her own nanny. When Rita came to Kate and asked that she get paid New York City rates (which were just slightly higher than California rates) for her time watching Logan in New York City, Kate reluctantly agreed. Kate and John thought this was a ridiculous request as the difference in the rates was so minimal. They were already paying for Rita to fly business class back and forth across the country, and they always made sure nanny Rita had her own hotel room separate from Kate and baby Logan while in New York City. They didn't really have a choice though. The precedent had been set early on by nanny Rita. And nanny Rita got what nanny Rita wanted.

Rita had the upper hand in the relationship. Kate and John were both extremely busy running and trying to grow their own businesses in the midst of having their first child, and so they let Rita run the show. It was a good thing that John was a Microsoft Excel wizard because he had to develop an elaborate spreadsheet to keep track of nanny Rita's multi-tiered payment schedule, which changed from week to week depending on the travel hours. Kate often wondered when exactly the payment rate should change? At the moment they crossed over into New York airspace? Or perhaps it was when wheels touched down at Kennedy Airport?

Although Kate and her husband John tried not to make the same mistake when they hired their second nanny, they kind of did. John, who worked in the tech industry, used his background in management consulting to put together a detailed PowerPoint presentation as to what type of nanny they should hire next. He even came up with a family vision plan and household brand in search of "Nanny 2.0," as he called her. Kate laughed out loud at her husband's attempt to use his business acumen to find a nanny for their family. She understood how John felt helpless and wanted to do everything he could to hire a better nanny—one that wouldn't boss them around. The PowerPoint and vision plan seemed to have been done in vain, because Kate and John's nanny number two, Alex, was a bossy nanny.

Nanny Alex came to Kate and John through a craigslist ad. She was a red-headed, bright-eyed British woman in her mid-forties who had two children in high school. Alex appeared to be a very hard-working woman. She was organized and exemplified a can-do attitude. Kate liked her immediately, as she reminded Kate a bit of herself. In the beginning, nanny Alex's organizing skills came in handy. Alex became a household manager of sorts. When Kate was at work and Logan was napping, nanny Alex went room to room, organizing the whole house. Kate would come home from work and find her house looking like an ad for The Container Store. She liked it—a lot. Until things got a little creepy.

During nanny Alex's time working for the family, Kate became pregnant with baby number two. John and Kate decided to learn the sex of their unborn child, and when they found out they were having a boy, Kate was excited to decorate a baby boy's room. After all, Kate was a decorator by profession, and she was pleased to have a new home project having already set up a baby girl's room for Logan. Seeing that Kate was extremely busy as always at work, nanny Alex offered to help Kate in setting up the new baby boy's room. Although Kate really wanted to do this on her own, she recognized that her time was constrained, and so she agreed to let Alex help out.

Kate showed Alex a few catalogs that she had been looking through with some ideas for the new baby's room. Kate thought Alex might also look through some of the catalogs for fun and to get some ideas that she would then share with Kate before acting on the ideas. Meanwhile, Kate had given Alex her credit card to run household errands, but she had explicitly told Alex only to use the credit card to purchase items on the family grocery store and Target lists. Kate thought she was making her life (and Alex's) easier by doing this. Alex had some issues with credit card debt in the past and could no longer have a card of her own.

Kate's water broke six weeks before her due date, and she delivered baby boy Patrick much earlier than expected. Kate ended up staying in the hospital with Patrick longer than originally planned. When she was finally released with her new baby, she was very excited to finally come home to her own house. Kate was surprised to find

Patrick's nursery all set up and decorated. While Kate was in the hospital, Alex had bought everything for the room. Nanny Alex had gone a little crazy online shopping with Kate's credit card. She had purchased items for the baby that Kate had never even heard of, including a warmer for the baby wipes and a toy turtle that lit up the whole room. Kate was overwhelmed by all of the stuff.

Who is the mother, not to mention the professional decorator? wondered Kate. Kate was the one who had repeatedly appeared on HGTV and decorated rooms and homes across the country that were featured in home design magazines. Apparently, though, she was not the boss of her own new baby's room. Her nanny was. When Kate confronted nanny Alex on the issue, Alex explained how she didn't see anything wrong with what she had done. She felt that she was in charge of the children and that meant buying what she wanted for the new baby's room. Kate ended up spending more time than she wanted to returning many of the items that Alex had purchased, including the baby wipe warmer and the giant light-up turtle. Nanny Alex soon became known as the shopaholic nanny.

More problems arose during Kate's maternity leave while she was home with little baby Patrick. While Kate nursed Patrick and cared for him while still trying to answer work emails, nanny Alex often took Logan with her to the playground or out to run errands. Nanny Alex liked to be out of the house when Kate was home, and Kate was happy to have her own space. Kate did get suspicious, though, when nanny Alex was out with Logan for hours and hours at a time. An errand or trip to the park turned into a whole day.

Since Alex was still using Kate's credit card for errands and outings with Logan, Kate happened to notice a charge for lunch on the card at a restaurant in Half Moon Bay—a beach town two hours away from their house in Northern California. Kate was amazed that nanny Alex took it upon herself to make the decision to take Logan on a long beach day trip without mentioning it to Kate. Nanny Alex wanted to be the one in charge of all decisions, and that would no longer work for Kate. Things soon came to a head, and it became clear to both Kate and Alex that there was only room for one boss in the family. Kate let Alex go.

Nanny Knows Best

Our fifth nanny, Alice, knew more about certain aspects of parenting and caregiving than I did. Because of this, she also bossed me around. And as was the case with our third nanny, Molly, I was fine with it. Nanny Alice changed up the television programming in our household. She explained one afternoon to toddler Joey and later that night to me that she didn't think it was appropriate for Joey to watch one his favorite television shows, *Caillou*. Alice recommended that he watch another show, *Little Einsteins*, instead. *Hmm*, I thought to myself after she mentioned this to me. I kind of hated Caillou. He was a whiny little character who never ever listened to his parents. I had thought about getting Caillou out of our house for a while, but I never had the guts to do it. Alice sure did.

Nanny Alice very calmly and thoughtfully explained to Joey that *Little Einsteins* was a much better show for him to watch. She assured him that he would like all the little characters in it and really love all of the adventures that they had together. Alice told me how the program promoted positive messages of kids working together, and that Joey would learn from it while laughing along with the characters in it. I was sold. The *Little Einsteins* kids sounded like the exact opposite of that whiny Caillou character, who was really getting on my nerves and Neil's too. Although Joey was initially a little sad over the programming change at home, he got over it pretty quickly.

Nanny Alice had her opinions on what was good and what wasn't good for our children, and she acted on them. I made a point in telling her that I appreciated her making these sensible decisions, but that we should still have an open dialogue about these matters as they came about. I think she agreed with me on some level, but she probably wanted me to stop talking as I was always very chatty with her. She just kind of yessed me. I think she knew that she was in charge of my kids no matter what, and deep down, I did too.

Jane, my college friend and the museum store director in New York City, knew that her nanny Lily was more knowledgeable than she was on many childrearing fronts. It was nanny Lily who was better at disciplining Jane's kids Helena and Oliver. So Jane let Lily take charge on that front. Nanny Lily employed the two-book rule in Jane's household. Lily would read only two books to Helena before naptime, and that was it. It didn't matter how much Helena begged and pleaded for more books or how big of a tantrum she threw, Lily would only read those two books. Nanny Lily explained to Jane that she had to stick to this plan at nighttime or the plan would backfire. Much like I did with nanny Molly and the pacifier, Jane learned the hard way that she had to follow nanny Lily's plan. Although Jane paid nanny Lily for her time with the kids, Lily was really more like Jane's boss.

Jane was more than happy to comply with nanny Lily's rules. Nanny Lily was in charge of what toys to buy for what age, what books to take out from the library, and what new foods the children should be trying. The situation worked so well for Jane and nanny Lily because Jane trusted Lily fully and completely. She knew that nanny Lily was a true professional, and that she had her kids' best interest at heart. In Jane's house, the nanny boss worked.

Rachel's Rules

ON BEING THE BOSS

When you hire and employ a nanny, you need to establish up front that you are the boss. That means you are the boss of the nanny, of your children, and of all major household decisions. But also establish that you want to keep an open dialogue—always. Issues will inevitably arise along the way, when it may become unclear as to who is the boss in one situation or another. This happened with nanny Molly and me in the case of the pacifier and nanny Lily and Jane in the case of the books before bed. In both of those instances, it worked out really well that the nanny was the boss. That's not always the case. Kate's nannies became too bossy in situations where they shouldn't have been.

I can look back now and can say with some distance and with some humor that some of our nannies became the boss of me. While it is funny to think about, the truth is that the parents really do need to be the ultimate bosses. I should have been clearer with nanny Alice that I was the one in charge. The nanny can have lots of power in certain areas, but she must always know that the ultimate decision-making power comes with the parent. Don't forget that.

❧ 7 ❧

Judgment Call

Good judgment is not necessarily something that can be taught or learned, either on the job or even throughout a lifetime. I try to surround myself with people who use good judgment. Neil is one such person. I can always count on him to make the right call, especially under pressure. When he was stuck with a flat tire on the side of the road late at night with our young son in the backseat tired and a bit frightened, he had the good sense to call me and wake me up so that I could go pick up Joey from the backseat of the cold car. My friends tend to use good judgment too. I trust them when they give me advice, make plans, and watch my kids during play dates and sleepovers.

I think of myself as a person who uses good judgment. I can properly assess a situation and make the right call, whether it's as simple as what to wear, what plans to make, or, more importantly, who to trust and who not to trust. The exception to this rule may just be in some of my choices in hiring nannies. I thought all of our nannies would use good judgment in any, if not most, situations in regards to caring for our children, but that wasn't always the case.

Bad Idea

Our first nanny Amy made one particularly bad judgment call when Joey was about a year old, and that incident still haunts me today. I sometimes wonder what I could have done to prevent the situation from happening, but I can't torture myself like that. I am just grateful that everything turned out to be fine. Because it could have been worse—a lot worse.

My office phone rang one day, and when my home number popped up on the caller ID, I thought it was unusual, but I wasn't too nervous. I picked up the phone and heard nanny Amy's distressed voice on the other end. She sounded like she was crying and definitely panicked.

"Rachel, I'm so sorry but Joey fell off the kitchen counter and now he has a big bump on his head." She started to really cry.

"I'm so so sorry. I understand if you want to fire me," said nanny Amy.

I took a deep breath. "Amy, calm down" I said. "Does he seem okay? Is he alert and acting normally?"

"Yes, he seems fine," she replied. "I've been holding him for a while and he calmed down."

"Okay. Do his eyes look normal? The pupils?" I asked, thinking about the possibility of a concussion.

"Yes they look normal, but he just has this big bump on his head," she said.

"Alright, I will come home to check him out. Be there in a few minutes." And with that, I hung up the phone and, as quickly as I could, explained to my boss Lisa that I had to run out for a few minutes to check on Joey. Lisa understood, and at that moment I so appreciated having such an understanding boss and having a job that was so close to home.

By the time I got home, Amy had calmed down and was standing in the kitchen holding Joey very close to her. The bump on his forehead was in fact as big as she had described, but otherwise he did look fine and seemed like himself. I held Joey for a while, and he babbled to me and smiled. I suspected everything was really going to be fine, but I did want to know exactly what happened.

Nanny Amy explained to me how Joey fell off of the kitchen counter onto the floor. She had propped him to sit on the counter as she emptied the dishwasher.

"You left him sitting alone on the kitchen counter?" I asked, trying not to sound as mad as I felt.

"I know, I know, I shouldn't have. I'm so sorry."

The three of us spent some time hanging out together until I felt things seemed status quo, except, of course, for the big bump on little Joey's forehead. We had a talk about how Amy had to make sure that Joey was not left unaccompanied like that ever again, even if it was just for a second. She agreed. I flashed back to the time a couple months before when baby Joey had fallen off the changing table as I reached underneath it for a diaper with both of my hands. But that happened on my watch. I could screw up my own kid. I'm the mother. But the person I was paying to watch him certainly could not.

I made a few calls as I drove back to work, first to my pediatrician's office. The nurse on the phone assured me that it really sounded like everything was just fine. We did the right thing in checking his pupils, he wasn't throwing up, and he was alert and happy. I still insisted on getting an appointment to have him looked at that night. Next I called Neil. He was amazed at what Amy had done, and was also really mad.

"What kind of person leaves a baby on top of a kitchen counter and then goes to unload the dishwasher?" he asked, truly perplexed.

"I know, I know," I said. "Amy said she'd totally understand if we fired her, but I really don't want to fire her. I think this was just one incident of bad judgment," I said as I defended Amy (the person who had allowed this to happen) to my own husband. Let's put it this way: if someone who worked for me in an office setting had put her number one priority, whatever that may be, in danger and neglected it like that, that could be cause for letting her go. Amy did just that. And in this case, the number one priority was my child—an actual human being. Not once did I ever seriously consider letting her go. The thought of finding someone new, a stranger, to watch Joey seemed scarier to me.

Our pediatrician examined Joey thoroughly that night and said he was absolutely fine. The bump would go away, and Joey would be no worse for wear (maybe not so much for his mother, and his nanny too). "The bump incident," as it came to be known, was forgiven, but certainly not forgotten.

Nanny number five, Alice, made a few bad judgment calls throughout the three years that she worked for us. One in particular also involved Joey's head, but was in no way as scary as the big bump. It involved a haircut—a very bad one.

I had asked nanny Alice to take Joey to the children's haircut place in town in the days leading up to his first day of kindergarten. Alice took the kids to the hair place and then promptly left upon seeing the long back-to-school haircut line. She had another idea—an at-home haircut. Alice brought the kids back to our house and proceeded to try out "a cool new look," as she later explained to me. She had seen it on a little boy at the playground and thought it looked really fun.

She found Neil's clippers and razors in our bathroom and proceeded to shave the lower part of Joey's hair down to his scalp. Then she just trimmed the rest of his thick, straight, dark brown hair around the edges. When I arrived home that evening, I was literally speechless. I am rarely, if ever, without words. It looked like nanny Alice had put a soup bowl around Joey's cute little head and then shaved everything outside of the bowl's diameter. I thought of the Jim Carrey character in *Dumb and Dumber*. That's what Joey looked like, only with bald patches down the back of his neck.

Then all I could think of was that his first day of kindergarten would be forever remembered in our family photographic history as the "bad haircut" day. The only saving grace was that Joey didn't seem to care. In fact, he kind of liked it. I finally managed to say something.

"Wow, that's some haircut, buddy," I said to Joey with a very forced smile.

"I know, Rach," said Alice before Joey could respond. "I did it myself. It's this cool new look that I thought would look good on Joey. He has such great hair."

He did have great hair. *At least he used to*, I thought to myself. Nanny Alice explained further how she opted out of the professional haircut and did it all on her own. Being as polite as I could, I thanked her for taking the initiative, and then calmly explained to her how she really shouldn't cut our kids' hair again . . . ever. I think Alice got the point, even though she still seemed pleased with her work. I was grateful that Neil didn't see Joey's hair until later that night when Alice was long gone. I'm not sure he would have been as polite as I was. We thought about shaving Joey's whole head so that it would all at least be even, but Joey didn't want that. And if we did that, it would be a big insult to nanny Alice and her hair-dressing capabilities.

We did nothing. I thought of my mother and how she used to say that the best thing about hair was that it always grew back. My mom had comforted me with this knowledge after I had cut my own bangs practically up to my forehead when I was five years old, and again when I got my hair cut very short after a bad perm in high school. Joey's hair eventually grew back, and we had it professionally trimmed evenly. Nanny Alice knew not to do home haircuts ever again. I wondered, though, about her judgment in the matter. I got it that she didn't want to wait in such a long line to get Joey's hair cut that day, but I would have thought she had the sense to wait before she cut my kid's hair, or at least asked me before she did it. Apparently not.

Nina, my curly haired friend, Philadelphia lawyer, and mom to three small children, also experienced a bad haircut and bad judgment situation with long-time nanny Liza. One day while walking home from her office to get her car to drive to a deposition, Nina spotted nanny Liza strolling her twin babies down the street in front of their house.

Always happy to sneak in a quick visit with her kids and with her nanny, who she had really grown to love, Nina leaned in to kiss each baby on the cheek. As she stood over the double stroller, she noticed that there was no hair sticking out of her daughter Sasha's winter hat.

"Liza," said Nina as sweetly and innocently as she could. "What happened to Sasha's hair?"

"Oh," responded nanny Liza, thinking nothing of it. "Her bangs were sticking out of her hat and she couldn't see that well, so I just cut them."

Interesting, thought Nina as she tried to keep it together. Sasha and Sam had just turned one, and had not yet had their first haircuts. A first haircut was a big deal—a really big deal. Nina wanted to be there for them. She even had the little pouches to hold the hair from their first haircuts marked "baby's first locks." *Where were those precious first locks? Did nanny Liza at least save them?*

Nanny Liza could see that Nina was not happy, but she really didn't mean any harm in cutting Sasha's bangs.

"I'm sorry, Nina," said Liza. "I didn't think you would mind. I just wanted Sasha to be able to see. Those bangs were making it hard for her." Nina couldn't really blame nanny Liza. I guess I couldn't really blame our nanny Alice either. Both ladies were trying to do their best, even if they didn't use good judgment. They didn't think it through.

Nina pulled herself together and drove to her deposition. By the time she got there, she couldn't keep it together anymore. Nina cried before she walked into the deposition. She had missed her daughter's first haircut. Nina comforted herself when she gathered the hair from Sasha's second haircut and placed it in the "baby's first locks" pouch. Only Nina, her husband Mark, and of course nanny Liza would know that they weren't the real first locks.

Are You Kidding Me?

While nanny Liza worked well for so long for Nina's family, her poor judgment became an issue more than once. Nina developed a schedule for nanny Liza so that while all three of the children were napping, Liza would clean the house. It seemed like a good idea, and usually worked out well. Until the day that Nina came home from work to find bleach spots on the chair and ottoman in the twins' room.

When she asked nanny Liza about the white spots on the blue furniture, Liza had a very honest answer.

"Sam woke up from his nap early, so he helped me clean, and he spilled the bleach in his room," explained Liza. Her answer perplexed Nina for many reasons. For one, nanny Liza was only supposed to be cleaning when the kids were asleep. Even if they were awake when she cleaned, the kids should not be the ones cleaning, and they most definitely should not be exposed to bleach in any way, shape, or form. Nina imagined that the situation could have been a lot worse, just like I did when our nanny Amy accidentally let baby Joey fall off the kitchen counter onto his head.

Nina thought for a minute about having to call poison control for a child who had ingested bleach. She was glad that the bleach only damaged the furniture and not the children, but Nina questioned nanny Liza's judgment again. She really couldn't imagine what she had been thinking that afternoon. Nanny Liza offered to pay to have the chair and ottoman reupholstered, and Nina took her up on the offer.

Nanny Rori, who worked for my friend Suzanne the social worker, became a little famous in Suzanne's family for not having the best judgment. Although Suzanne worked extra hard to make sure she gave nanny Rori explicit instructions as best as she could, and nanny Rori worked hard in trying to follow the instructions, there were issues.

Suzanne and Scott's house was really cold in the winter. They tried as best as they could to regulate the temperature and insulate the house more, but it was just one of those things that always seemed to be a problem. Suzanne came up with a solution in purchasing space heaters for her childrens' rooms, and they worked really well. Suzanne instructed nanny Rori to turn the space heaters on in the childrens' rooms before she put them to bed. Suzanne worked late one night each week running group sessions for cancer patients at the hospital. Scott's commute and long hours made it hard for him to be home for bedtime. And so nanny Rori was in charge of bedtime once a week.

Rori knew the routine: The kids should wash up and brush their teeth. Rori then read to the kids in their rooms, tucked them in, and turned on the space heaters so they would have a nice and cozy good night's sleep. Nanny Rori had it all down, and Suzanne was grateful for having a nanny that could be so flexible and handle bedtime.

One evening in November as Suzanne came home from her group at the hospital, she was reminded how unseasonably warm it was when she didn't even need a jacket as she walked to her car. *The temperature must have gone up to near 70 degrees*, thought Suzanne as she turned on the air conditioning in her car. It was indeed an Indian summer as the weatherman reported on her car radio. Suzanne's house felt especially warm that night. When she went to check in on her kids before saying goodbye to nanny Rori, Suzanne could actually see the sweat dripping off her son's brow. Nanny Rori had put on the space heaters in the kids' rooms that 70-degree night.

When Suzanne asked nanny Rori why she had the extra heaters on when most people were using air conditioning that night, nanny Rori explained that she was following instructions. *Fair point, I guess*, thought Suzanne. Nanny Rori was told to put the space heaters on every night, and that is exactly what she did. Rori clearly did not think outside of the box. Suzanne wondered, though, if she was thinking at all. Suzanne had another instruction to add to her endless list for Rori: when it's really hot out, don't turn on the space heaters.

Suzanne's third nanny, Karen, was also known for making less-than-stellar judgment calls. Young nanny Karen was always too open with Suzanne, and saw very few boundaries between her personal and professional life. She felt way too comfortable around Suzanne, and this made Suzanne uncomfortable. Suzanne hired nanny Karen to watch her kids on her late night at work after nanny Rori could no longer do it.

On many of these late nights at work, Suzanne felt emotionally drained, having just led group therapy sessions with cancer patients. Suzanne just wanted to come home and unwind in front of some mindless television, or go to sleep. Yet, dealing with nanny situations usually took the place of her idea of a relaxing night. Suzanne came home one night surprised to find nanny Karen wearing a shirt that she hadn't come to work in. In fact, it was not her shirt at all, but rather the bright yellow oversized favorite t-shirt of her husband Scott.

Not really sure what to make of the wardrobe change, Suzanne asked nanny Karen about it.

"Oh," explained Karen. "I got my shirt wet while bathing Ryan, so I just went into your closet and grabbed one of Scott's shirts. I hope you don't mind. It's so cozy. I love it!"

Of course it's cozy, thought Suzanne. *It's Scott's favorite shirt!* He wore it almost every weekend and took pride at how nicely worn-in it had become. It felt just as soft as Suzanne's son's favorite baby blanket. Suzanne knew Scott wouldn't be thrilled with the impromptu borrowing of such a favorite wardrobe staple.

"It's okay," said Suzanne, "but please bring it back next time you are here."

"I will, I definitely will," replied nanny Karen. Suzanne wondered how many times she would have to ask for the shirt again before it was returned to its rightful owner, as Karen tended to be a bit flaky when it came to remembering things like this. The shirt was eventually returned, but Scott spent a few weekends wearing his second-favorite t-shirt, which was nowhere near as comfortable. Suzanne was amazed that her nanny had made the call to go in to their closet and take an item of clothing out like that, and then to wear it in front of her so casually. Suzanne couldn't imagine what nanny Karen was thinking.

My business school friend and interior design professional Kate, who employed bossy nanny Alex, had a strikingly similar wardrobe issue with nanny Alex. Kate wondered what kind of judgment nanny Alex used during the "yoga pants incident," as it came to be known in her house. Kate was on maternity leave after giving birth to her son Patrick, and she was still working on getting into pre-baby shape. One day Kate ran out to the gym in her husband's old sweatpants while nanny Alex watched the kids. When Kate came home, she couldn't believe that Alex was standing in front of her wearing Kate's favorite form-fitting yoga pants—the ones that she loved but could no longer fit into. That made the situation even worse for Kate.

Apparently baby Patrick had spit up on Alex's jeans that afternoon, and just like nanny Karen, nanny Alex had gone into her boss's closet and changed into the coziest, and in this case too, Kate's most favorite item of clothing. Kate was not happy at all. She questioned Alex's judgment, her inability to draw the line at what was appropriate, and she was just plain mad to see her nanny fit so nicely into clothing that she wished she could wear. Kate had a chat with nanny Alex that day and learned a good lesson from the yoga pants incident. Kate implemented a new rule for future nannies that she laid out as clearly as possible. She added "must bring change of clothes" to her list of written-out nanny requirements. That was all it took. Lesson learned.

Rachel's Rules

ON JUDGMENT

Good people make bad calls. It doesn't mean they are bad people. It just means they sometimes don't always think everything through before they act. This seemed to have been the case for nannies Rori, Karen, and Alex. The same could be said for nannies Alice and Liza. They didn't mean any harm with the bad haircuts. They really believed they were being helpful.

Of course nanny Amy didn't mean any harm in leaving Joey on the kitchen counter while she emptied the dishwasher, but I probably should have questioned her judgment more back then. I should have at least considered firing her. After all, my son's wellbeing was at stake. The problem was, though, that I was too in-the-moment to step back and think about her judgment and how that would affect her job performance. I think Neil really did want to fire her, but I was already too close to her, and I thought Joey was too.

As in so many cases, employing a nanny is not like employing someone in an office environment. It's easy for the parents' judgment to be clouded when thinking about their own nannies and their decision-making processes. I sometimes wondered if there was any way I could figure out if a potential nanny had good judgment during the interview process. I thought about asking case questions during interviews, much like my husband did during his interviews for candidates who wanted to work at his firm right out of business school. He would give the candidates scenarios, asking them what decisions to make regarding a certain business matter, and then evaluate the candidate's judgment based on his or her answers. I thought about asking nanny candidates what they would do in any given situation, but the answers always seemed so obvious to me that I would feel awkward even asking. Case in point: When emptying the dishwasher do you, A. leave the baby unattended on the kitchen counter; B. hold the baby the whole time; or C. let the dishes be and focus on the baby? Sometimes the answer is quite obvious in theory, but less so in practice.

When it comes to finding nannies with good judgment, you need to be as clear as possible with your instructions, encourage your nanny to ask questions (there should be no such thing as a stupid question when it comes to your kids), and know your limits. Understand what you can tolerate as far as bad judgment calls and what is just too much to take. Then be ready to act accordingly based on your own parameters.

⤚ 8 ⤙

Busted! The Secret Lives of Nannies

We never had a nanny cam. I didn't even consider getting one. I am generally a very trusting person, and I thought that installing a nanny cam would be a violation of our nanny's privacy. I also thought it would drive me crazy and distract me from getting any work done. I've heard stories of people watching their nanny cams all day long while at the office. *Don't you hire a nanny so that you can go to your place of work and actually do your job?*

I think that when you hire a nanny or really anyone, you need to establish a level of trust between yourself and that person, and you need to let go of some control. Having said that, I do understand that many people may feel otherwise. There is a reason that you can scroll through amazon.com for hours searching through what seems like an endless supply of nanny cams. You can buy a nanny cam hidden in an alarm clock, a coat hook, and even a water bottle. Spying on your nanny is big business. As our kids got older though, it became apparent to us that we wouldn't need a nanny cam. The secret lives of our nannies came to us via other means.

Busted

Neil discovered a little secret about nanny number three, Molly, when I was in the hospital having just given birth to our baby girl, Rebecca. Rebecca arrived three weeks early and caught us all by surprise. I had worked a full day in my office less than twenty-four hours before I went into labor. Rebecca was a tiny baby. As Neil liked to say, "She wasn't fully cooked." And so she was kept in the NICU for several days. I stayed at the hospital a bit longer as well, as I had an emergency C-section because Rebecca ended up being breach. That left Neil in charge of Joey at home, and he was as happy as was I to have nanny Molly continue to work for us throughout my maternity leave.

One day he returned home from a visit with baby Rebecca and me in the hospital, only to discover the back door to our laundry room wide open with the dryer on. Just as he was about to take a look outside through the open door, nanny Molly came inside and swiftly shut the door behind her. She told Neil that she had the door open for some air with the dryer running at full blast, and she assured Neil that Joey was sleeping soundly upstairs. She explained that she could hear him all the while on the baby monitor from downstairs. Neil later told me that nanny Molly reeked of cigarette smoke, and he knew she had been outside smoking just then.

Being almost as nonconfrontational as I am, Neil did not say anything to nanny Molly about the smoking. He was exhausted from his crazy-as-ever work schedule and taking care of Joey while baby Rebecca and I stayed in the hospital. Perhaps more than anything though, Neil really liked nanny Molly, and much like me, he didn't want to stir things up just then. Neil did go outside after

Molly left that night to look for cigarette butts, of which he found none. He comforted himself and me, too, in saying that at least she had cleaned up after herself. Nanny Molly was just as neat in her smoking outside as she was in her housekeeping inside. So from that point on we knew that nanny Molly was a smoker. We never had an incident again and assumed, but really just hoped, that she wouldn't smoke on the job again after being caught by Neil. We never knew the truth and never would.

My friend Nina's nanny Liza was also busted, but not by a family member like our nanny Molly had been. Nanny Liza was narced out by Liza's neighborhood dry cleaner. Nina received a call from the across-the-street dry cleaner one day at her law firm. Thinking that she had forgotten to pick up some shirts, Nina answered the phone in the midst of reviewing documents on her desk.

"Nina, I know this sounds kind of strange, but I wanted to let you know about something that I saw today," explained the dry cleaner. "I saw your nanny moving her car from your driveway to the street."

Okay, thought Nina as nanny Liza often parked in their driveway when she couldn't find a spot on the street, and that was fine with Nina.

"Sasha and Sam were standing out on the sidewalk while she moved the car. I just thought you should know," said the concerned dry cleaner, who then quickly ended the call. Nina could tell that the dry cleaner felt uncomfortable and didn't want to get involved in the situation any more than she already was.

Nina finished her work for the day in the office, all the while knowing that she would have to discuss the matter with nanny Liza when she got home. Nina thought that there had to be a reasonable explanation. And according to nanny Liza, there was. Nanny Liza explained to Nina that she wanted to move her car out of the driveway and onto the street before Nina returned home from work so that Nina could have her spot in the driveway. Nina appreciated her consideration. Nanny Liza was always very thoughtful.

"I do appreciate that," Nina said to Liza. "But why were the twins standing outside on the sidewalk? They could have run into the street or something." The family lived on a city street. It was a quiet one, but a city street nonetheless. "And where was Zach?" asked Nina, thinking of her baby son.

"Zach was inside taking a nap. I wanted to make sure that I could see the twins while I moved the car, and so I made sure they stood still on the sidewalk," explained Liza in her usual very caring manner. Nina didn't press the issue much further. She just made sure that nanny Liza knew not to do it again. Nina appreciated her neighborhood dry cleaner telling her what was going on that day, and she wondered what else she didn't know about. She tried not to go there. Those thoughts have occurred to just about every working mother who at one point or another has left her children in the care of someone else.

One such mother was my friend Michelle, the marketing research professional who moved to Pennsylvania from Atlanta. Much like Nina, Michelle received a surprising report about her nanny Nora from her next-door neighbor in Atlanta. One Saturday afternoon, Michelle took her two young children over to the neighbor's house for a play date. While catching up over coffee, the neighbor expressed her concern for nanny Nora's financial troubles. Trying to play it cool, but also trying to figure out what was going on, Michelle inquired further.

It seemed that nanny Nora had asked Michelle's neighbor to borrow some money while she was over at her house earlier that week. The neighbor lent her the money as she felt bad for Nora, and she knew how good she was with Michelle's children and with hers too. The situation did not sit right with Michelle. She and her husband Ed had lent nanny Nora money over the years in addition to buying her two cars and helping to bail her out of jail. Michelle was initially mortified that nanny Nora was asking her neighbor for money. The neighbor assured Michelle that it was perfectly fine with her. She trusted nanny Nora, just as Michelle did. The incident inspired yet another talk between Michelle, Ed, and nanny Nora.

Technology Works

I was surprised one day at work to get a Facebook friend request from nanny number five, Alice. Facebook was relatively new, at least to me, back in early 2009. I didn't know that nanny Alice had discovered it, and I certainly didn't know that she was browsing around on the social network while she was supposed to be taking care of my kids. I looked at my watch when the request popped up on my computer. Joey was still at school and Rebecca was most likely napping, but she was still at work. I guess you could have said the same thing for me. Even so, it wasn't the smartest thing for her to send to me, her boss. I would never send a Facebook request to my boss during work hours. I probably wouldn't send my boss a Facebook friend request at all. I hesitatingly accepted nanny Alice's request later that night, and didn't say much about it.

Soon I had to. I started to check Facebook at night, and could see that Alice had been posting all throughout the day while she was at my house with my kids. I went on to our home computer in our kitchen and very easily pulled up nanny Alice's browsing history. I discovered that she had been on Facebook all afternoon. She was on my computer, looking up friends from long ago and posting quotes and updates on what she was doing—with my kids!

I had to bring up the Facebook issue with nanny Alice, especially after I learned that a teacher at my childrens' preschool had been fired after a similar incident. One mother who was Facebook friends with the teacher discovered that the teacher was posting to Facebook during the middle of the day, when she should have been teaching in the classroom. Apparently the teacher was taking lots of breaks in the teacher's lounge in order to find time to devote to her social networking habit. The whole situation struck me as a bit ridiculous. My mother never had to deal with Facebook posts from good old Mrs. Dougherty. I secretly wished for that simpler time.

I explained to nanny Alice that she needed to be focused on my children when she was with them and that she couldn't be browsing around on my computer all day.

"I'm sorry, Rach," she said, "but the kids were playing nicely together, and I think they need that independent time."

What? Of course I know that they need independent playtime, but not so their nanny can catch up with old high school friends on Facebook while I'm paying her to watch them.

I took a deep breath and explained this as nicely and calmly as I could, but I'm not sure nanny Alice really thought that she was at fault. She had been with us for well over two years at that point and felt comfortable, way too comfortable, around me. I know that I was partially to blame, as I never wanted there to be any tension between the two of us. I made things very easy on nanny

Alice because I wanted things to be easy for me. In hindsight, that wasn't the smartest thing to do. I said my peace and explained very clearly to Alice how I could see everything she did on my computer and on Facebook. I didn't mean to get all Big Brother on her, but I was trying to make a point. There were fewer Facebook posts from her during the day, but there really should have been none. If my boss had initiated that conversation with me, I would have deleted my account altogether.

Nanny Maria also got busted by technology. Maria worked for my friend Anne, the pharmaceutical executive and mother to three children. Anne, her husband Richard, and their young kids really liked nanny Maria. She was referred to the family through their housekeeper, and although her English wasn't great, and the family never knew her last name, they trusted Maria and developed a solid and loving relationship with her. Anne and Richard trusted people implicitly. They are do-gooders and have been known to take people under their wings to help them along. When Anne's parents offered to stay with her children for a week so that she and Richard could get away just the two of them, they chose to go to Africa and help children in an orphanage. I so admired her for doing that, and not sitting on a beach for a week with her husband like most people (including myself) would be inclined to do.

Anne and I initially bonded on the playground when our lookalike daughters became good friends at just two years of age. They were drawn to each other, as were their mothers. Anne and I often ended up talking about what we wanted to be when we grew up as we discussed the pros and cons of our current jobs and our struggles to make it all work, most especially with childcare. I always found

Anne to be inspirational in what she did professionally and in her volunteer work. She was one of the reasons I became more involved in volunteering for the nursing home where I now sit on the board. If Anne could travel to Africa and help build a well for kids halfway around the world to have clean, healthy water, then I could certainly carve out some time to be with the residents of the nursing home and raise funds for the building. Anne put things in perspective for me when I needed it most. She reminded me that we were lucky to be born in the time we were and in the country that we were. She took nothing for granted, and I tried to do the same, most especially when I was around her.

Anne worked four days a week at her office in New Jersey, and since she had very small children who weren't old enough to go to school, Anne told Maria that she was not to drive the children anywhere. They had enough to do in the home and at the nearby playground, which they could walk to. Nanny Maria agreed to this rule, no problem. Only one day it became apparent to Anne and Richard that Maria wasn't following through on the rule. Nanny Maria proudly showed Anne and Richard pictures from her phone of the kids sitting together on an oversized sofa.

Cute, thought Anne. *But whose couch is that and what are those unfamiliar walls and pictures in the background of the photo?* Richard wondered too. When Anne asked Maria about where they were, she explained that she had driven the kids to her friend's house over in the next town. Maria didn't think she had done anything wrong.

Did she forget about the rule, or did she ever even know about it? Anne was never really clear if nanny Maria understood everything that she told her. Language was an issue. Anne reiterated her rule about not driving the kids anywhere. She trusted that Maria would follow the rule this time, but as was the case with so many other mothers and nannies, she never really knew the truth. How could she?

The Nanny Cam

For those parents who want to know, or think they want to know, what is going on at their homes all day while they are at work, there is the nanny cam. My friend Emily and her husband Brian tried it out when they lived in Dallas before moving back to Pennsylvania where they both grew up. I wasn't surprised to hear that they had the secret camera, as Brian was very into technology. He was the first person to tell Neil and me about Sonos, so that we could listen to music in any room in our house on wireless speakers. Brian was our unofficial information technology specialist. His real job was in the retail business and it took him out of the country sometimes for weeks at a time. Brian wanted to know what was going on at his house on these long travel stretches. He wanted to spy on their nanny who cared for his three girls. Our own IT specialist very easily set up the nanny cam.

Emily was not as sure about the nanny cam. She worked in schools as a therapist and was at heart more of a trusting person than Brian was. Like my friend Suzanne, also a social worker by trade, Emily tried to see the best in people and help them in their struggles, whatever they may be. When Neil and Brian were both traveling for work, Emily often had me over to her house for dinner with the kids. It was great. The kids played outside or in the basement while we enjoyed a glass of wine, her famous grilled chicken salad, and solid adult conversations. I don't think Emily has ever called me by my real name. Instead she addresses me as "Love," "Friend," or, my personal favorite, "My Dear." She can get away with using those terms of endearment for her friends. I don't think I ever could.

During one of Brian's long trips to China when he was curious about what was going on at home, he logged onto his computer, which he had set up to give him remote access to the nanny cam. Brian was beyond shocked at what he saw. On his computer screen was a picture of a large woman, a stranger to him, washing her very large breasts over his kitchen sink. The woman then patted down her breasts with the family's favorite, super-absorbent Williams-Sonoma dish towels, folded the towels, and placed them right back on the kitchen counter. Brian was beside himself. He was looking at his kitchen sink through the camera and wondering who the hell the breast-washing woman was and where were his kids?

He quickly dialed Emily's cell phone number, not wanting to call the home phone and speak to the breast-washing stranger standing in his kitchen. Emily was in a meeting at one of the schools where she worked. When the meeting ended, she was disturbed to see nearly fifty missed calls from Brian. *What the hell is going on in China?* she wondered.

She called Brian right away and got an earful from him.

"Um, Emily honey, there is some strange woman in our kitchen washing her very large breasts in our kitchen sink," Brian reported. "Where the hell are the kids? Who is this woman? What the hell is going on?" asked Brian in a full-on state of panic.

"It's okay honey," Emily explained. "Calm down. I can explain everything." And she really could. Their regular nanny had called out sick, but Emily was able to find a backup in the neighbor's nanny. The neighbor's nanny had just come back to work after having given birth to a new baby boy. She had brought her breast pump with her, and Emily figured out that she must have just pumped and cleaned herself off in their kitchen. The girls were upstairs asleep, Emily assured Brian, as it was their naptime. Brian wasn't really aware of the schedule, especially while in China and fixating on the breast-washing stranger in his own kitchen.

Emily and Brian were eventually able to laugh about the giant misunderstanding. Emily did make sure to thoroughly wash the Williams-Sonoma dishtowels after she returned home from work. The couple later discussed how the nanny cam can be a good thing, but can also cause moments of panic like the one that Brian endured. Yes, you do want to know what goes on in your house while someone is watching your children and you are at work. But you also have to take each situation on a case-by-case basis. And as Emily and certainly Brian discovered, there are some things that go on in your house that you may not want to know about, and definitely not see for yourself.

Kids Do Talk

The good news, or the bad news, depending on which way you look at it, is that eventually your kids will get older and they will talk. They will report back to you on their day's events, from the most exciting things to the most mundane, including what their nanny did. I felt a bit like a secret spy when I first figured this out. Joey was five years old when he told me about the songs on the radio he heard while in the car with nanny number five, Alice.

One day while I was driving Joey to soccer practice, he asked me to change the radio to 97.1. *Hmm*, I thought. *Joey's branching out.* I was happy to get a break from the incessant pop music that my kids could never get enough of. I wondered what kind of music they played on 97.1. I figured it out pretty quickly. It was Christian radio. The station broadcasted very catchy and very pleasant music, but I didn't think it was so appropriate for my children, Jewish children, to be literally singing the praises of Jesus Christ. Yes, my childhood nanny Mrs. Dougherty had taken my brother and me, two Jewish children, to church services with her, but that didn't seem to bother my parents. The Christian radio bothered me.

I was happy that Joey let me know about his new radio listening habits. I talked to nanny Alice and explained to her that I didn't feel comfortable having my children listen to that station. It was definitely an awkward conversation, but I felt it was a necessary one. I tried very hard not to offend nanny Alice because I respected her religious beliefs, and felt that she should be able to listen to whatever she wanted on the radio, but just not when my kids were in the car. I likened it to Neil listening to Howard Stern (and he loves to listen to Howard Stern) with my kids in the car. I'm not sure that was an appropriate analogy, but I was struggling to make sense and not offend her. I'm pretty sure nanny Alice got the point as Joey never again asked for the station.

Joey and Rebecca also reported back to me on their lunch outings with nanny Alice. One Saturday while running errands in the local shopping center, the kids asked if we could get Wendy's for lunch.

"No, kids," I said. "Wendy's is not so good for you. You know I don't like you to eat fast food."

"Alice lets us eat Wendy's," said Joey.

She does, does she? I felt so all-powerful in having my children unknowingly act as two little nanny spies. I asked more questions, treating my children as if they were eyewitnesses to some kind of crime, knowing full well that I may have been crossing the line. But then again, nanny Alice had done something that she knew she shouldn't have. I got about as much intel from my hungry five- and three-year-olds as I could. It seemed that nanny Alice had taken the kids through the Wendy's drive through for lunch on several occasions on days when they were home from school. She must have paid for their lunches with her own money, which I sort of felt bad about for just a minute. Nanny Alice covered up her tracks nicely. There was never any evidence of the fast food in our trash. I wondered where she threw it out.

I had to confront nanny Alice on the issue. She backpedaled as much as she could and explained that it was only on very few rare occasions when she was in a bind for food and the kids were so hungry while they were out. I let it go as best as I could. Nanny Alice came to understand that my kids could tell me everything, and that she really had to follow the rules—hopefully all of them. I began to wonder less about what went on when I was at work, as I knew that my kids were turning into great nanny narcs.

My friend Nina's twins Sasha and Sam also began reporting back on their days with nanny Liza as they got older. Nina was pleased to know more about what went on at her house, but it was tricky. She didn't want to outwardly turn her kids into little spies, and she didn't want to infringe on the level of trust that had been established between her and nanny Liza.

One day while driving around a part of the city that they rarely visited, Sam mentioned to Nina that nanny Liza had driven them up to this neighborhood one day. *Really*, thought Nina. She wondered why, and so she asked Sam more about that day. He explained how nanny Liza had taken the kids up to that neighborhood and had left them in the car while she ran in to pick up food at the Boston Market. Nina cared less about the food and more about the fact that her nanny had left her kids in the car in an unfamiliar neighborhood while she ran into a store.

Nanny Liza would never put the kids in harm's way on purpose. She truly loved them, and Nina knew this, but it still wasn't the best move. Nanny Liza explained to Nina that she could see the kids the whole time, and that the car door was locked. This made Nina feel a tiny bit better, but she still had to stress the importance of never doing something like this again. She hoped, much like I did, that nanny Liza would think twice about doing something like that since she knew the kids would report back to her.

Rachel's Rules

THE SECRET LIVES OF NANNIES

You will never know about everything that goes on with your children and your nanny while you are at work. It's just not possible, even with a nanny cam. You need to accept this fact and have enough trust in the person that you hire to care for your kids. Once you do accept this, you should also know that your nanny will do things with your kids that you wouldn't do. She is not you, and that's just the way it goes.

Try to be on top of the goings-on in your childrens' lives with your nanny by having an open dialogue, and continue that conversation with your nanny every day that you see her. Encourage her to be open and honest with you, but don't get too Big Brother on her. Use technology to the extent that you feel comfortable to keep tabs on your nanny, but don't let it take over your life. Otherwise, you will never get any work done. And isn't that why you hired a nanny in the first place? Case in point, eventually I stopped checking Facebook to spy on nanny Alice. I put as much trust as I could in the conversation that we'd had about it. Also know that eventually your kids will report back to you, and then you will know more than you ever wanted to know.

❧ 9 ❧

Only One Mother

In the last couple of weeks of my mother's life, she gave me some very sound advice. As I sat with her in the hospital bed set up by the hospice nurse in my parents' bedroom, we had some really good conversations. We talked about big-picture stuff, wondering how and why she got sick so young, what it meant to be a good parent and the course that our family's life had taken. We also talked about the little stuff and the day-to-day worries of life. Even though she was so sick, my mother still focused on what she knew best—being my mother.

I tried to take her mind off of how lousy she felt and talked a lot about baby Joey. I mentioned my concerns over the very real possibility that our first nanny Amy would leave one day, and one day soon.

"Rach, your nanny is replaceable," she said in a very soft voice. "Joey knows you are the mother. Don't ever forget that." That was some of the best advice that anyone has ever given to me. I thought about it a lot over the course of employing many more nannies. I still find myself giving that advice to other working moms.

Kids Know

My mother was right. When nanny number two, Ellie, and nanny number three, Molly, came in and out of our lives within the course of one year, I tried to keep that advice close to my heart and to my mind, but it was hard. I was very worried about two-year-old Joey when we began the search for nanny number four. I thought for sure that I had screwed him up for life with the revolving nanny door in our house. I wondered if he would develop trust and abandonment issues? He must have been wondering who he should listen to, who was in charge, who would stick around? Who were all those ladies taking care of him?

In reality, though, Joey only had one thing on his little two-year-old mind: Bob the Builder. You know, the animated contractor from the popular television series on Nick Jr. and later PBS. Joey became obsessed with Bob, Wendy, Scoop, Muck, Dizzy, and my favorite, Farmer Pickles. He couldn't get enough of the show and all of the mini action figures that made up the construction crew. I happened to mention his fascination with Bob to Joey's preschool teacher one day in the midst of explaining my worries about finding a new nanny that Joey could connect with. The teacher suggested that when I hire the new nanny, I buy some Bob the Builder action figures and give them to the nanny to give to Joey. Then, she explained, he would feel at least some kind of connection.

I liked it. And so, after we officially hired nanny number four, Julie, I gave her a few new Bob characters to give to Joey, explaining my strategy. Neil thought I was a little nuts. Nanny Julie probably did too. I kind of thought I was. Regardless, the plan worked. I introduced nanny number four, Julie, to Joey as a big fan of Bob the Builder.

"Look Joey, Julie likes Dizzy too!" I explained to him as I could actually hear the desperation in my voice. Joey seemed content. Bob or no Bob, I think deep down Joey was secure enough to know that although he had new nannies coming and going, I would be there every single day for him. Although I didn't care for him all day long, he knew I was the mother, and that I wasn't going anywhere. I sensed this in the sweet smile I got from him every workday when I came in the door. He was happy to see me, but he also knew he would see me. I was the mother, the only one.

It Still Hurts

On an intellectual level I understood that my kids knew I was their one and only mother. That didn't change the fact that it sometimes hurt on an emotional level when I let the nanny take over to care for them. Especially on those occasions when it seemed like my kids were better off with the nanny than they were with me. Joey and Rebecca took direction from nanny Alice way better than they ever did from me. I was green with envy as I watched Rebecca sit still and not make a sound as nanny Alice brushed out her knotty hair one morning. Brushing out Rebecca's hair always brought on a fight between the two of us, and Rebecca never let me put her hair up in pigtails. Nanny Alice did her hair in pigtails, braids, French braids, whatever hairdo she fancied. I was amazed. Rebecca looked adorable. I was happy that she looked so cute, but also jealous that she would only let our nanny make her look that cute. Who was I? Just the mother . . .

I arrived home on the earlier side one evening to find the kids setting the table for the dinner that nanny Alice was making for them. I was impressed. My five and three year olds were taking part in preparing for dinnertime in a very real way. I was happy that Alice had them helping out like that. Then I wondered, *Why didn't I think of that?* If I had, the kids probably wouldn't have been as agreeable to the whole idea as they were with nanny Alice. She made taking care of my kids look so easy and so fun. It was never that easy for me.

Nanny Alice sometimes sensed my envy, and she was very understanding about it.

"Rach, it's my job to have fun with the kids. I am getting paid to do it," she said one evening to me. "You have to take care of the kids and do everything else too. I can just focus on them," nanny Alice explained. She did have a point. When I was with the kids, I also had to do laundry, grocery shop, make dinner, make the family plans, check my work emails, and try to be a good wife, friend, daughter, and sister. Nanny Alice could, for the most part, just focus on taking care of the kids for nine hours a day, three days a week. I appreciated her honesty with me, and perhaps even sympathy for me. She validated my insecurity on the issue, and I never really considered myself to be insecure—about anything. I thank my mother for instilling me with a strong sense of self. I guess it didn't translate so well into motherhood though, at least back then.

My jealousy of nanny Alice's ease with my kids only grew as I began to feel more and more that I was missing out on the fun stuff that she got to do with them as they got older. I couldn't attend their preschool back-to-school picnic as it was smack in the middle of a workday when I was running a meeting. Nanny Alice was happy to go in my place, and I so appreciated that. She had been with us for a couple years at that point and knew the childrens' friends, their teachers, and many of the other mothers and nannies. Alice had fun at these events. She took lots of pictures for me of the kids getting rides on the pony and playing in the little bounce house. I loved to check out their painted faces (Alice's too) at the end of the day when I got home, but I secretly wished that I was the one there with the kids helping them to choose between the mermaid and the fish, or the soccer and the basketball face paint designs.

My friend Nina, the Philadelphia lawyer, was also lucky to have a fill-in mother in nanny Liza. Nanny Liza attended a few of Nina's childrens' school plays when Nina couldn't be there because a client needed her at the office. Nina's kids loved nanny Liza and happily accepted her as the substitute mother on these occasions. Still, the jealously was there for Nina. After all, it was that feeling of missing out years before that brought Nina to tears at the deposition because her nanny had given her daughter her first haircut.

Jane, my good friend from college and the New York City museum store director, knew how Nina and I felt. Jane's daughter Helena had grown very attached to her nanny Lily over the years. There were many occasions when Jane came home from work to find Helena asleep in the stroller in the apartment. Both Jane and nanny Lily agreed to leave her in the stroller and not wake her from the late afternoon nap. When Helena woke up, she often cried out for nanny Lily. Jane understood why it happened. Helena wondered where she had gone while she slept. The intellectual understanding of her young child's confusion still didn't ease the tiny pain Jane felt when she heard her daughter cry out for "Li, li," the nickname turned term of endearment that Helena had given to her beloved nanny.

Power Struggle

When more than one adult is in charge of a child, there will be struggles. They happen between mothers and fathers, parents and grandparents, and most definitely between mothers and nannies. These power struggles sometimes developed between Lori, my friend the accountant and mother of two young girls, and her nanny Tricia. This first became apparent to Lori after she received a text from nanny Tricia while away on a business trip. "I think you are giving in too much to the girls" appeared on Lori's phone just as she was walking into a meeting. Lori didn't know how to respond. She felt like she was being judged by her nanny, and that Tricia was playing the power card with her. Lori understood that nanny Tricia spent significantly more time with her children during the week, and she knew them very well, but she also knew that she was the parent and should have the ultimate say on these kinds of issues. Wasn't she ultimately the one in charge of her own children?

Each woman thought she was right in the midst of their power struggle. Each woman felt she had the best interest of the children at heart. Each woman also wanted to take credit for the childrens' achievements. Lori was surprised to see a Facebook post on nanny Tricia's wall one evening: "I'm so proud of Abby's artwork. She was so careful and took her time and she's only four!" *Interesting*, thought Lori. Tricia's writing about my daughter for all of her Facebook friends to see as if Abby is her own child. Lori felt slighted. Clearly there was some tension between mother and nanny. Nanny Tricia took pride in Abby's work as she should, but Lori wanted to share in her pride. At the very least, she thought that she deserved to be tagged in the Facebook post. Lori wanted some kind of acknowledgement in her daughter's budding artistic ability. It takes a village, and the mother is certainly one of the leaders in the village. In Lori's view, Tricia was taking too much credit. Although Lori has tried a few times to initiate a larger discussion about this struggle, the issue remains.

Rachel's Rules

ONLY ONE MOTHER

As my mother so wisely told me, there is only one mother, and children know this from the time they are babies. Remind yourself of that when you feel envious, jealous, or sad that you are missing out on pieces of your childrens' lives. No one can ever replace you. You are the mother. Say it again and again. It helps.

And don't be so hard on yourself. It's perfectly natural to feel insecure, jealous, or even angry about the fact that someone else gets to spend more time with your kids during the day. Try to channel those feelings into more positive ones. Be the bigger person. Feel grateful and appreciative that you have found another person who loves your children almost as much as you do. When your child makes a connection to your nanny like mine did with Alice and Jane's did with Lily, embrace that connection. That's a good thing. Your child will inevitably develop feelings for their nanny, so be happy when they are good ones.

You must also accept the fact that you are going to miss out on some things. You are a working mother, and you just can't be there for everything. No one can. As a side note, for you and your family's sake, figure out what events you can be at and really make an effort to get there. There are certain things that you really don't want to miss. For my family, it was Joey and Rebecca's holiday show at preschool every year. I managed to always get there. But when you can't be there, feel grateful once again that you have someone else in your nanny that can be there for those times. I always knew the kids had fun with nanny Alice at the back-to-school carnival, and that made missing out on the event hurt less. It really did.

☙ 10 ☙

A Teacher Too

Everyone remembers their favorite teacher. You know that one teacher who you respected, admired, liked, and with whom you had a real connection. I was lucky enough to have a few favorite teachers.

In elementary school, it was Mrs. King. She had so much energy and she made learning fun, like when we got to make our own weather forecasts and predictions in a science lesson. Mrs. King and I shared a love of Doritos, and when you are in third grade that's big. In high school, it was Mr. Cantlay. He made the pages of Jane Austen's *Pride and Prejudice* come to life, as he passionately read the thoughts and feelings of Mr. Darcy and my favorite character, Lizzie Bennet. I think of Mr. Cantlay whenever I make a connection to a character in a book that I read now as an adult. And in college, it was Professor Faust who took me and the rest of the class with her on a journey through the history of the American South. She taught me how to analyze conflict and to make connections between history and the present in ways I could have never imagined. I am lucky to have had those teachers.

Little did I know that I would one day find teachers, and good ones at that, in the nannies that I employed. Some nannies taught me invaluable parenting lessons while others tried to impart some of their own unique skills to me—like gardening and home decorating. Each of our nannies also taught our kids many wonderful lessons and skills. I am forever grateful that my children found teachers in our nannies.

For the Parents

Our baby nurse Jackie was my first childrearing teacher. I called her the baby whisperer as she had her own special way of connecting with baby Joey, and, years later, baby Rebecca. I hoped she would teach me all of her tricks.

Jackie was a strict teacher. There was to be no cuddling and cooing with the baby during the middle of the night feedings and changings. Otherwise, baby Joey would want to stay up all night and play, and we had to teach him the difference between daytime and nighttime. Joey also had to be woken up every three hours during the day for a diaper change and a feeding. He needed to get enough nourishment during the day so that he would sleep at night. This information seemed so obvious once Jackie explained it to me, but honestly I would never have thought of it on my own.

Jackie needed to write down Joey's ever-changing eating and sleeping schedule. I found an old half-used spiral notebook from my economics class in graduate school for her. It was buried in my boxes of notebooks and textbooks from high school, college, and business school that I still kept in our basement. I held on to them, thinking I would need to revisit them one day, but I never thought that it would be for recording my baby's eating and sleeping schedule.

"I hope this is okay," I mentioned to Jackie as I handed her the notebook with the word "Econ" crossed off. I wrote "Baby Joey" right below.

"No problem," she replied. That was a typical Jackie response. Everything was "no problem," said emphatically with her strong Trinidadian accent. I learned to say it too.

Jackie later told me that the last family that she worked for had bought her a laptop to record their baby's schedule. My old flimsy notebook seemed to pale in comparison. I learned about some of the other families she had worked for and that her nurse friends had helped out. It became a who's who in the baby celebrity world. I felt like I was browsing through the "Star Tracks" pages of *People* magazine, one of the magazines that I used to work for in New York, as she recounted the goings-on inside the Hollywood homes of moms with new babies.

I felt a little spoiled to have the huge help in Jackie as I was still home, especially as I learned that she was the baby nurse to the stars, but I look back on that time as a real learning experience. Jackie taught me how to take care of my baby. I am sure I could have figured it out on my own, but she certainly made it easier on me. Especially since the first diaper I ever changed in my whole life was my own child's. When I babysat back in high school, it was only for older kids.

Jackie also guided me in figuring out the whole work-life balance issue, which I struggled with from the moment I brought baby Joey home from the hospital. She could read people really well, and I was no exception.

Jackie knew after only a week with me that I should work outside of the house, and she told me so. Even as I was immersed in breast-feeding (and struggling with it), changing diapers, and trying to figure out how to swaddle my new baby, she could tell that I needed to get back to my career. Maybe it was because I talked to her constantly and asked her a million questions. She could tell that I needed those outside adult connections.

Jackie watched me try to figure out how to get a baby onto a schedule, and also deal with the reality of a very sick mother, who she figured out very quickly did not have much time left. Jackie told me about her family back in Trinidad, all seven of her children and many more grandchildren whom she regularly sent money to from here in the states. Even though we spent just a few weeks together, I felt a very strong bond with her. I mean, how many complete strangers come and live with you, eat with you, see you topless, and help your new baby latch on to your breast, all the while listening to you cry about your dying mother and your feelings of being overwhelmed by just one new baby?

So yes, I was a bit of a mess in those postpartum days, but I was happy to have Jackie with me. The perspective she brought to my situation then, and even now, is never far from me. I often think about the struggles she went through to become a baby nurse in the United States, and the support she provided to her own family at home in Trinidad, not to mention the countless families like mine that she helped at the sweet, yet difficult, time of bringing home a newborn. I am forever grateful to have had her as another great teacher in my life. Baby nurse Jackie is right up there for me along with Mrs. King, Mr. Cantlay, and Professor Faust.

Nanny Alice became a teacher of sorts to me. Alice noticed my lack of a green thumb during the first spring that she was with us. I planted my red geraniums in two pots right out by our front door, just like my mother used to do, and they promptly died several weeks later. I let the dead flowers sit there for a few weeks, not wanting to deal with the mess right in front of my house and my nose.

"Rach," nanny Alice said to me one evening after I came home from work. "Would you mind if I planted some pots for you? I have some ideas for your front yard."

"Sure," I responded, feeling thankful that nanny Alice had some sympathy for me and my inability to figure out which plants need sun, partial sun, partial shade, or full shade. I was clueless.

We made a plan to meet at the Home Depot Garden Center one day after work so that Alice could actually teach me about what to buy and plant and not just do it all for me. *Teach a man to fish . . .* I thought. I was so impressed with nanny Alice's knowledge of plants, flowers, soil, and mulch. We had the kids with us, and Alice got them involved, asking for their input on color and size. We selected impatiens, calendulas, petunias, pansies, and coleus.

Nanny Alice introduced me to a whole new world beyond my mother's geraniums, which apparently needed full sun. Who knew? I saw Alice eyeing more flowers after we had selected the items for my pots, and I offered to buy them for her. Alice was very much appreciative, and I was happy to get them for her. When nanny Alice and I worked well together, we really worked well together. I was thrilled that we had formed a connection above and beyond the children. It gave us more to talk about. I left the plants and soil out in our front yard overnight, and the next morning, nanny Alice explained to me exactly what she would plant that day with the help of the kids while I was at work. Her arrangements looked beautiful and they didn't die—they bloomed even more and grew and grew. I became confident enough to plant my own pots the following year. I still think of nanny Alice when I'm at the gardening center, planting or watering my flowers.

Nanny Alice also taught me a few things about home improvement on the inside of the house. She saw my messy desk area in the kitchen and came up with a great solution for my never-ending piles of papers and pictures.

"I'm going to make you a bulletin board," nanny Alice announced one day.

"Okay," I said, a bit thrown off by her latest project, "but I haven't had a bulletin board since I was a kid," I responded as I thought back to the beat-up old cork board with the painted sunshine and rainbow on it above my desk in my childhood bedroom.

"Don't worry, Rach," Alice explained. "It will be so cute. You'll love it, and I'll show you how to make one yourself." And she did. Nanny Alice bought a large piece of corkboard at Office Depot, very pretty raspberry colored fabric at JoAnn's Fabric store, and showed me how to make a very beautiful and functional kitchen bulletin board. Nanny Alice measured the board so it would fit perfectly into the area above my kitchen desk. It looked amazing. The kitchen finally looked complete. I imagined Alice could get her own show on HGTV: *The Home Decorating Nanny.*

Our third nanny Molly taught me a skill that I could have never mastered on my own. And believe me, I tried for a long time. Nanny Molly showed me how to successfully fold a fitted sheet. My whole life, I wondered why the fitted sheet always stood out from the pile of neatly folded sheets in our linen closet. The edges just never stayed together.

"No worries," said nanny Molly as she folded Joey's fitted crib sheet, pulling from the middle of it so that the sides naturally just fell together. Once Molly showed me her trick, I had it made. Nanny Molly changed the look of my linen closet forever.

Nanny Liza taught her boss Nina other invaluable lessons. These lessons went well beyond the basics of folding a fitted sheet, although I still say that's a great life skill. Nanny Liza taught Nina how to be more adventurous with her own kids, as nothing stressed nanny Liza out. She had a very mellow attitude about life, and was a true free spirit. Nina didn't operate that way. She was very organized and even regimented with her kids. With three small children at home, and a demanding legal practice, Nina craved the rules and routines that made her life run smoothly. Nanny Liza taught Nina how to relax a little bit with the rules.

Most days, nanny Liza came to work at Nina's house without a plan for what to do. She would take Nina's three young children all around the city in their strollers and on the bus, exploring new parks, playgrounds, and museums. These unplanned days were some of the children's most fun and memorable ones. When nanny Liza reported back to Nina on their adventures, Nina began to think that she could let loose a little bit more with the kids, and that it was fine to not always have a plan and to go with the flow and see where the day takes you.

Nanny Lily also taught her boss Jane in New York City to have more fun with her children. Jane didn't have a lot of confidence in her mothering skills. She sometimes felt that her children were better off with nanny Lily. When Jane was with her kids, she often felt that she was just trying to get through the next step: dinner, bath, bedtime, and then wake up and start all over again. Over the years though, nanny Lily showed Jane how to play with her kids, how to laugh with them. Nanny Lily opened Jane up to a whole new world with the children. She taught her how to be silly, that it was okay to just lie on the floor with them and make them giggle.

And the Children Too

When another adult outside of your family is charged with taking care of your children on a regular and frequent basis, it's inevitable that she will teach the children new things. In most cases, that adult is coming from a different background, has different skills, different stories to tell, and will bring new perspectives to any situation. That can be a really good thing.

Our nanny Alice was a teacher to our children in every sense of the word. In addition to teaching Rebecca to crawl and Joey to appreciate the values of the *Little Einsteins* television geniuses, she taught our kids about good manners and about getting along with each other when it was the last thing they wanted to do. Neil and I were their first teachers when it came to manners. I made my kids say please and thank you ad nauseam until I couldn't stand the sound of my own voice, but it worked. They were polite kids, and I took a lot of pride in that. Nanny Alice did too, and she should have. She reinforced the lessons in manners every day.

Nanny Alice made sure the kids were appreciative of everything they had, and most especially of each other.

I always knew my kids loved each other deep down, but some days I wondered just how deep down I had to look to find that love. They fought—a lot. And it was often over the dumbest things, like who got to sit behind which parent in the car, and who got to hold a bigger part of the book that they were reading together. Nanny Alice had no patience for these petty arguments. Where as I got involved immediately and often yelled at my kids, nanny Alice gave Joey and Rebecca the space and time they needed to work it out on their own. She explained her strategy to me, and I saw that it worked.

Nanny Daisy, who worked for our close friends Leigh and Fred, was from Peru and only spoke Spanish to Leigh and Fred's baby daughter Daphne. Although Leigh was the teacher by profession, nanny Daisy became Daphne's first language teacher. Daphne was bilingual by the time she was three years old.

Nanny Daisy took a liking to the family puppy, Harry, and trained him like a soldier. He was the most well-behaved dog on the block. Soon, though, Harry the dog only followed commands in Spanish. Leigh and Fred laughed as they found themselves with a dog that didn't understand English. He only sat upon hearing "*sentarse*," and handed his paw to nanny Daisy when she said "*pata*."

In California, where many kids were already speaking English and Spanish, my friend the interior designer Kate hired her third nanny, Flora, whose first language was Portuguese. Nanny Flora taught Kate's daughter Logan her native tongue and, before long, Logan was fluent in Portuguese just like Daphne was in Spanish. Kate and her husband John were pleased that Flora had taught their daughter her native language, especially because it was Portuguese and not Spanish. Their kids would be differentiated in a good way by becoming fluent in another language. Kate and John realized how ridiculous their thinking seemed, but they were still proud.

Nina's nanny Liza taught her daughter Sasha how to sew when they made Sasha's Halloween costume together. Nina could barely hem a pair of pants, and she was so happy that her nanny could help her daughter learn a skill she had never taken to. Emily, the school therapist who had lived in Dallas, employed a nanny who also showed her girls how to sew, and she sparked their creativity. Emily's nanny brought the girls to the Dollar Tree and the local arts and crafts store where they picked out fabrics and fun décor, and then designed and made their own costumes just for fun. Emily was more than pleasantly surprised to return home from a long day at work and watch her daughters put on shows for her in full costume under the direction of her nanny.

Back in New Jersey, nanny Franny, who took care of my childhood friend Ellen's young children, did in fact deliver on her promise to teach the kids the days of the week through her wardrobe. Franny did actually wear a different colored shirt for each day of the week, and before long, Ellen's baby daughter Natalie knew that Tuesday was blue and Wednesday was yellow. Ellen would have never thought of anything like that, and she so appreciated the effort and the lessons learned.

Nanny Cynthia became the second nanny for my friend Anne, the do-gooder and pharmaceutical executive. Cynthia was a gym teacher during the school day, and after school let out, she watched Anne's kids. Nanny Cynthia showed the children that exercise was fun through their dance parties in the basement with all the neighborhood kids. Cynthia also took the kids on botany tours and made botany books with them. And every holiday season, nanny Cynthia baked cookies with Anne's kids and helped them organize a holiday cookie exchange with their friends.

Rachel's Rules

A TEACHER TOO

When you have a nanny who teaches you and your children new things, embrace it. Learn all that you can from her. If it had not been for nanny Alice, I would still have dead flowers in my front yard and messy piles of paper on my kitchen desk. If not for nanny Molly, my fitted sheets would still be balled up in a pile in the linen closet. More important, though, are the invaluable lessons that our nannies taught me about childrearing. In many cases, the nanny is the expert in the field and can bring her experiences from other families to help yours.

Don't be upset when your nanny gets through to your children more than you do. It's easy to get a little frustrated when your kids listen better to your nanny than they do to you, but try not to go there. I worked hard to happily watch Joey and Rebecca's good behavior in front of nanny Alice. It gave me hope that they could get along better with each other at all times.

Appreciate all the new lessons and skills that a nanny will teach to your own children. There are so many opportunities for your kids to learn every day with your nanny. Think of their time together as a bonus in home-schooling. But make sure that these lessons and values are aligned with what you want your children to learn.

∾ 11 ∾

You Can't Make This Stuff Up

I've always subscribed to the belief that the truth can be stranger than fiction. In fact, that was part of the impetus for telling these nanny tales and writing this book. My friends always had stories to share with me about the crazy adventures they had with their nannies. So many of these stories ended with the phrase "you can't make this stuff up." And the truth is that you really can't.

The Evening News

Michelle, the marketing research professional who had moved to the Philadelphia suburbs from Atlanta, was completely caught off-guard in the process of hiring Tracy, the woman she thought would be her first nanny. Tracy had answered an ad that Michelle placed on Care. com, and the two women hit it off during the in-person interview. Tracy seemed to be a very caring, engaging, and energetic young woman to Michelle when they met. Like many of our young nannies, Tracy got right down on the floor to play with Michelle's young daughter. Michelle later checked Tracy's references, and they were excellent, as she had expected them to be.

Michelle and her husband Ed intended to hire Tracy as their full-time nanny, but they wanted to put one last test in place by having Tracy watch their daughter Hannah one Saturday night while they went out to the movies. Tracy was up for it, and they agreed upon the night and the time for the nanny test run. When Tracy didn't show up on time that Saturday night, Michelle was a bit annoyed but didn't think much of it. Tracy had told Michelle that she would be away on vacation during the week leading up to that night, so Michelle imagined that perhaps Tracy's flight home had been late or she got caught in what was always tough Atlanta traffic.

Once Tracy was officially a half hour late, Michelle sent her a text asking where she was. No response. Michelle started to worry. She called Tracy, and the phone went straight to voicemail. Michelle expressed her concern when she left a message for Tracy, but by that point she was really annoyed. Nanny Tracy was not making such a great first impression on her test run night. Michelle was also disappointed with herself, as her self-imposed love affair with nanny Tracy was starting to fizzle. She began to realize that she couldn't hire Tracy as their full-time nanny if she didn't show up for work on time and didn't return her texts or calls. After a few hours, Michelle and Ed gave up. They stayed in with the kids that night and were only slightly comforted by the fact that they didn't order and pay for their movie tickets in advance.

Ed was just about to turn off the television in the bedroom before they went to sleep, when Michelle became intrigued by a story on the screen.

"Hang on, Ed," said Michelle. "What's going on there? It looks kind of crazy," she said as her eyes became focused on the story being broadcast from downtown Atlanta not far from their house.

The newscaster was covering a large fight that had broken out at a party in a downtown hotel where several local sports figures and celebrities were in attendance. The party had gotten way out of hand, and two young female party-goers had gotten into a physical fight. In the midst of it, the women had actually fallen out of the hotel window and on to the street below a few stories down. Michelle recognized one of the women. It was nanny Tracy.

Michelle couldn't believe it. Neither could Ed. Before Michelle could process what had happened to her future dream nanny, the news clip was over. It was on to the next story. She understood that Tracy would not be her nanny, and she wondered if Tracy would be okay. Tracy looked like she was in pretty bad shape from the little that Michelle could see on the television. Over the next few days, as Michelle began her search for another nanny, she left several messages on Tracy's phone expressing concern and asking if there was anything she could do.

Eventually Michelle got a call from Tracy's sister with an update. Tracy was initially in critical condition after the fall, but she made great improvements faster than the doctors had expected. Tracy would need a lot of physical therapy, but she would be fine in the longrun. She returned home to Tennessee to recuperate near family. Michelle appreciated the call and was glad to know that Tracy would be fine. She still thinks of nanny Tracy from time to time, imagining what could have been and mostly remembering never to assume anything when someone doesn't show up for an appointment. You never know what could have happened.

The Matchmaker

While my childhood friend Ellen's nanny Franny appeared to be a prim and proper Mary Poppins type caregiver, complete with a Welsh accent and lessons on manners, she did have another side to her. Ellen first noticed this other side when they were having work done on their house in New Jersey. Ellen and Rob decided to finish their basement and convert it into a playroom for their growing family. They hired a handyman named Tom to help them do the work. Tom came with glowing references from Ellen and Rob's neighbors. Soon, nanny Franny was glowing on the days Tom came to the house to work on the basement.

Ellen started to take note of nanny Franny's growing interest in handyman Tom as Franny asked Ellen which days Tom would be coming to work on the house. Franny masked her curiosity under the guise of wanting to plan the childrens' nap schedules around the loud hammering coming from the basement. Was it just a coincidence that on those days when Tom worked in the house, nanny Franny came to work in nicer-than-usual clothes and bright red lipstick? Ellen thought not.

Nanny Franny did indeed have a crush on handyman Tom, and she wasn't shy about it. Ellen worked from home on Fridays, and when she came into the kitchen from her home office, she noticed nanny Franny bringing lunch to Tom in the basement. Ellen got nosy and started to find any excuse to leave her home office more than usual—an extra cup of coffee, a glass of water, a bathroom run—so that she could watch the mini soap opera unfold in her own home. Apparently Tom, a really nice and hardworking man in his early sixties, had a girlfriend, but he told nanny Franny that it wasn't going so well. Franny, a divorcée in her fifties with three grown children, really got into the ins and outs of Tom's troubled relationship.

Ellen learned through her eavesdropping, and eventually straight from the source, nanny Franny, that Tom and his current girlfriend did not have such a great sex life. Tom wasn't happy anymore, and with a little push from Franny, he broke it off with the girlfriend. Franny was right there to listen to Tom's troubles and ease his loneliness. Ellen definitely noticed a spark between her nanny and her handyman. She was happy that she could be an involuntary matchmaker of sorts, but she also wanted to make sure that her children were well cared for, and that her basement was finished on time.

The Joint

My friend and neighbor Diane, the speech pathologist and mother to three young children, employed nanny Jeannie for several years before she stumbled upon one of those "you can't make this stuff up" stories. Nanny Jeannie was a great influence on Diane's children, and she ran Diane's house way better than Diane ever could have. Diane used to say that she went to work so that nanny Jeannie could organize her life. And yes, nanny Jeannie did cross the professional to personal line on more than one occasion, but Diane and Justin had come to terms with that. "Nobody's perfect," Diane and Justin repeatedly told themselves.

Nanny Jeannie was always very open and chatty with Diane and Justin, so much so that Diane often found herself sneaking out of the house just as Jeannie was walking in the door so that she could get to work on time. There was one conversation, however, that Diane and Justin could not avoid, although they later wished they had.

One evening as Diane put together a quick dinner for her family and Justin paid nanny Jeannie for the week, Jeannie mentioned to Justin that she had an extra joint of marijuana given to her by a friend. She wondered if Justin might be interested in purchasing the single joint from her. Justin had to think before he spoke. *Did our nanny just try to sell me drugs?* he wondered to himself. *And does it really count as drug dealing if it's just a single joint?*

"No thanks," he calmly responded to nanny Jeannie, wondering all along what made Jeannie think that he smoked pot. He didn't.

"Just thought I'd ask because I don't smoke pot," replied Jeannie.

"Neither do I," said Justin, this time a bit defensively. "What made you think I did?"

"I don't know," answered Jeannie. "You just seemed the type."

When Justin retold the story to Diane later that night in the privacy of their own bedroom, Diane was able to laugh it off, but did note the craziness of the situation. Their nanny tried to sell them a joint, they politely declined, and then they all went on with the business of the night. Nanny Jeannie would be back bright and early on Monday morning, ready to take care of their children. They couldn't make that one up.

The Name Change

Pharmaccutical executive Anne's nanny Maria was very kind and caring toward her three young children, Ava, Erin, and George. Nanny Maria got to know the children pretty well over the years, and often made up her own little nicknames for them. Anne thought this was cute, just like I did back in the days when our baby nurse

Jackie called our newborn, five-pound baby girl Rebecca "Tiny." Anne soon wondered, though, about where the nicknames had come from and how long they would stick around.

It wasn't long before nanny Maria had actually renamed Anne's middle child, Erin. One day, Maria asked Anne about Erin's middle name.

"It's Angelina. She was named for my Aunt," explained Anne.

"That's beautiful," replied nanny Maria, and Anne didn't think much more about the brief conversation.

Maria did. She soon started calling Erin "Angie," and then only referred to her as Angie in front of Anne. Anne spoke to nanny Maria about this a few times, explaining that her daughter's name was not Angie. It was Erin, and that was what she should be called. These conversations didn't really seem to phase nanny Maria. Erin became Angie. Anne and Richard got used to it. The extended family and neighbors were kind of confused when Maria called Erin by her new name, but eventually they got used to it too.

For the two years that Maria worked for Anne and Richard, they felt like they had another daughter with another identity. She had a different name and perhaps a secret life that she led with nanny Maria. They still hear from nanny Maria now, six years later, when she sends the children a holiday card addressed to Ava, George, and, of course, Angie.

The Housekeeper

My friend the marketing professional, and unofficial nanny mentor, Stacey, found herself in an unusual situation with her longtime and beloved nanny Mariella. Over the years, Stacey had come to know nanny Mariella pretty well. After all, it was Stacey's husband Phil who brought Mariella home from the hospital after she had given birth to her first child. Mariella got to know many of the people who came in and out of Stacey and Phil's home on a regular basis, and she was quick to form an opinion on them. One such person was Stacey's housekeeper.

Mariella thought that the housekeeper's cleaning skills left something to be desired, and she found herself pitching in a lot to make up for the less-than-stellar job that the housekeeper was getting paid to do. Mariella took action. She reported back to Stacey on what was going on while Stacey was at work, and she had a suggestion for how to make things better. Mariella's good friend, Lina, was also a housekeeper, and, in her opinion, would be great for Stacey and Phil.

Stacey was game to hire Lina. She trusted Mariella and was impressed that she was taking action to improve their household. On the advice of her nanny, Stacey fired her housekeeper and hired her nanny's friend to clean her house. It was a great decision. Stacey and Phil's house never looked better.

Rachel's Rules

YOU CAN'T MAKE THIS STUFF UP

Just when you think you've heard it all, you realize that you haven't. And when you hire and employ a nanny who develops a long-term and often very close relationship with you and your family, you will hear and see even more. Your nanny will inevitably feel close to you— closer than you've ever felt toward any person you've ever worked for. Funny things will happen. Crazy things will happen. Anything and everything will happen. Go with it.

The key is in how you deal with these often-ridiculous situations. Take a page from Michelle, Ellen, Diane, Anne, and Stacey. Laugh about these instances when you can. Most times, these stories end up being really funny, even if that doesn't seem to be the case when you are living them. As my mother used to say, "They'll make for good dinner party conversation one day." They always did for me. If you ever feel truly uncomfortable, then of course address the situation head on, but everyone is different, and you should know your limits. Anne got used to her daughter's new name for the time that nanny Maria worked for her. Diane and Justin still trusted their nanny Jeannie despite the joint proposition episode.

❧ 12 ❧

Getting Dumped

Who likes getting dumped? No one. I don't care what anyone tells you while trying to console you after you've been dumped by a boyfriend, a girlfriend, or anyone, it's always better to be the dumper than the dumpee. I figured this out when my college boyfriend dumped me. I studied in London during my junior year, and my boyfriend and I agreed to stay together and do the long-distance thing. Before I left for London, I thought about breaking up with him so that I wouldn't be tied down to anyone when I was studying and traveling abroad. He convinced me otherwise, as he declared his undying love for me.

That love died down during my six months abroad. I came home to what I thought would be a fun reunion weekend with him, but he had other plans. That weekend turned into a long and painful two days of me getting dumped by him. It was bad. Although I knew that we had grown apart, and the breakup was better for me in the long-run, I was really pissed that he was dumping me. I had always thought it would be the other way around.

The same holds true for all of the nannies that dumped me. Each of them left for something else—a new job that was better suited for what they really wanted to do, a pregnancy, a health crisis, and the list went on. Although rationally speaking, I knew that in each case they didn't really have a choice but to move on. And just like when my college boyfriend dumped me, I knew that in the long-run I would be just fine. More importantly, I knew that my kids would be fine. That didn't change the fact that it still hurt.

We Will Never Know

I can't imagine how difficult it was for our first nanny, Amy, to tell me that she would in fact be leaving us. That's how it felt. Like she was leaving us—not quitting, not taking another and much better job opportunity, but leaving us. Abandoning baby Joey and their gym class and their walks, robbing me of a sense of security from having someone that I knew and trusted (even with the bump incident) to watch my child. After nearly two years of working for us as our nanny, Amy took a job in marketing for a financial services company. It wasn't what she wanted to do or was even interested in doing, but she needed a real job. She needed more money, and she also needed healthcare benefits, as she couldn't stay on her parents' healthcare plan forever.

Nanny Amy gave me six weeks notice, which was more than generous. She didn't know then that Neil and I were trying for baby number two, and when she did give notice I suspected that I was already pregnant. I remembered that advice that my mother gave me while practically on her deathbed that my nanny would be replaceable. I repeated this to myself over and over again.

Even after nanny Amy stopped working for us as our daytime nanny, she continued to babysit for us a couple

Saturday nights a month, so it wasn't like we would never see her again. That helped to ease the pain. Amy had fun with Joey as he grew into a toddler, and she even took care of our baby girl, Rebecca, who came along when Joey was a little over two years old. Amy was good with both kids. We had known her for over three years at that point, so we asked her to come along with us on our week-long family beach vacation.

We figured Amy could act as a parents' helper on the trip. We suspected that taking a toddler and new baby to the beach had its own challenges. We also hoped to sneak out for a couple of adult-only dinners on the trip, and we knew Amy could watch the kids at the rented beach house on those nights. She agreed to the set-up, and she wrote down the dates when I gave them to her, a good three months in advance.

The night before the vacation, I called Amy to confirm all of the details. She would meet us at our house the next morning, and we'd all drive down together to Long Beach Island for the week. It all sounded good, and Neil and I were excited for our first real family vacation. Amy seemed excited too. We even talked about how many bathing suits she should bring. I imagined her taking baby Rebecca back to the beach house for a nap, and then Neil and I would stay at the beach for the afternoon and play with Joey in the waves and in the sand. It was going to be great.

As we packed up the car that Saturday morning, I heard the phone ringing as I ran inside the house to grab a stack of towels for the trip. A bit surprised to see that it was Amy's parents' home number, I picked up.

"What's up?" I asked. "Getting all packed up?"

There was a long pause on the other end of the phone.

"I'm so sorry Rachel, but I can't come to the beach with you guys," she said.

"What? Is everything okay? What's going on? Are you okay?" I asked, feeling very concerned and also very surprised.

"I just can't go. I can't explain. I'm so sorry," said Amy. And with that, she hung up.

I ran out to the driveway to tell Neil what had just happened. We talked about it for a bit and decided it was best not to call her back and probe her on it. We had no idea why she had canceled like that, and literally at the last minute. We spent a decent amount of time on that beach vacation wondering why she never showed. We never heard from her after that.

It's been seven years now, and several nannies, since I received that phone call from Amy, and every now and then Neil turns to me and says, "I wonder whatever happened to Amy? Why did she cancel on us?"

Our best guess is that Amy really did have a lot of social anxiety—more than we had ever noticed. She held her own with kids and babies, but looking back on our experience with her, she never felt comfortable around us or really with any other adults. She also seemed to never want to let us down, and we think that's why she agreed to come to the beach with us so far in advance. We think that when it came down to it, she couldn't deal with living with us for a week on vacation. Perhaps she felt too anxious about the whole thing. Maybe she thought she could do it, but then felt the anxiety and backed out at the last minute?

Either that, or she had a strange allergy to the sun that she couldn't explain. Perhaps she lived a secret life as a double agent and had to leave the country suddenly?

There are many theories that we now just have to laugh about, otherwise we'd go crazy. We trusted this person with our children, our babies, over the course of three years, and one day a strange phone call ended it all.

The Real Job

Our second nanny, Ellie, who had earned her degree in elementary education, had been with us for the whole summer after nanny Amy left. Once September rolled around, Ellie told us that she'd be with us for at least another year. She did not get a teaching position as we had thought would be the case. I looked forward to having the stability of having her around as I prepared to have a baby that winter. The stability ended pretty abruptly one afternoon.

It was a Thursday, and I was in the car with Joey when I got the call. I actually remember the date—September 8, my mother's birthday. A few of my mother's friends had just taken Joey and me out to lunch, as they were thinking of us on the day. I was so appreciative to have her friends as part of my life. They acted as surrogate grandmothers to Joey, showering him with two-year-old birthday gifts for his upcoming September birthday, just a few days after my late mother's birthday.

It was nanny Ellie calling, and she sounded really excited and happy.

"Rachel, I got a real teaching job. I'm so excited," she reported. My heart sank.

"Wow—congratulations," I said. "When do you start?"

"Tomorrow. I know it's short notice, but my sister Nancy can watch the kids until you find someone else. I'm so sorry, but I am so excited for this teaching job," she went on to explain.

I pulled off the road into a gas station. I wasn't feeling so great and I didn't want to get into an accident. It took me a few minutes to digest. I got the particulars on Ellie's sister, who had actually watched Joey a couple times throughout the summer when Ellie had to switch a day with us and the other family that she was also working for. I comforted myself with that backup plan, but really I was pissed. How could Ellie leave us like this after only a few months, and with less than twenty-four hours' notice? I had never heard of anything like that. I held it together because I didn't have a choice.

Nanny Ellie appeared to be the one in charge, and I had to go along with her plan. At least she had one. I got the particulars on Nancy, and then just really wanted to get off the phone as quickly as possible. I was sort of disgusted with the whole situation, with Ellie for doing this and with me for letting it happen. Had I done something wrong? She had seemed committed when I hired her.

My friend Suzanne the social worker's longtime nanny, Rori, also left her for another job, and it caught Suzanne by surprise. While Suzanne knew deep down that Rori would not be a lifelong nanny, she secretly hoped that Rori would work for them until her kids were much older. Nanny Rori was not perfect, but she had grown on Suzanne, and Suzanne's kids loved her. Suzanne felt that she had taught Rori a lot about taking care of kids, and that Rori had, in many ways, grown up with the family.

Suzanne thought that perhaps Rori would go back to school one day and become a teacher, or maybe a guidance counselor. Suzanne took pride in having trained Rori in the field of childcare and in fostering her passion for working with kids. So when nanny Rori announced to Suzanne one day that she would be leaving the family for a job working for a caterer, Suzanne was not only surprised but also disappointed. One of the things that drew Suzanne into the field of social work was her desire to help others. She always tried to find the best qualities in each person and help them find their true calling if possible. Nanny Rori was no exception.

"A caterer?" Suzanne asked, trying not to sound as surprised and hurt as she really was.

"Yes," said Rori. "It's for my friend's business. I'll get to learn how to make some really cool dishes, the hours are good, and so is the pay."

"Okay," replied Suzanne. "We are going to miss you so much. Don't forget about us. You know that you can always come back and babysit for the kids whenever you want to," said Suzanne, feeling abandoned and also kind of desperate. She sounded like one of those girlfriends who gets dumped by her boyfriend, and then in a knee-jerk reaction, tells him that she would take him back at anytime. *Pathetic*, thought Suzanne. At the same time, Suzanne couldn't in her wildest dreams imagine Rori working for a caterer. This was nanny Rori, the same person who needed step-by-step instructions on how to work the toaster oven.

Stacey's fourth nanny, Gina, also left to pursue a job in another field. For nanny Gina it was psychology. Gina was studying for her degree in the field while she worked for Stacey, and was very open about it. Stacey knew that nanny Gina would one day get that real job, but she didn't think that she would be the one to find it for her.

Stacey managed to get herself dumped. As the school year drew to a close and nanny Gina was preparing to graduate, Stacey received an email from a friend who she knew worked as a psychologist. Stacey noticed the signature on her friend's email, which listed her place of work. On a whim, Stacey asked if the friend's psychology practice might possibly be looking to hire. They were. Stacey's friend interviewed her nanny Gina and offered her a job in the office. Stacey was very happy for nanny Gina. She had prepared herself to get dumped.

The Surprise Pregnancy

About a month after I had gone back to work after my maternity leave for baby Rebecca, our third nanny, Molly, called me the night before she was to come to work. When the phone rang, I had just stepped out of a relaxing bath as I congratulated myself on getting the two kids to bed early while Neil was away on a business trip. I would have the whole night to read, watch a movie, and just have some time to myself. I felt like I was getting the hang of being a working mom with two kids at home. I shouldn't have picked up the phone.

"Rachel. I can't believe this, but I'm pregnant. We didn't plan this. It was a major surprise," said Molly on the other end of the phone.

"Wow, congratulations," I said. What else could I say? I could feel the tension creeping back up in my neck. *So much for the long, hot bath.* I started to do the math in my head to try and figure out how much longer she could be our nanny. I flashed back to our interview with nanny Molly. She had told us that she didn't want kids for many years. I had so many questions and things that I wanted to say, but none of them were appropriate. I didn't have to ask them, though, because she told me just about everything that night on the phone.

"I started on this new birth control pill," Molly explained, "and I guess it didn't work." *Oh do you think* so, *doctor?* I never really understood those surprise pregnancies. I mean I know that sometimes (like 1 percent of the time) the pill really doesn't work, but in most cases it's because people forget to take it, don't take it correctly, or they take an antibiotic at the same time and don't read the label. I managed not to get pregnant on the pill for nearly twelve years. Why couldn't my nanny do the same? Molly went on to explain that she would continue to work for us throughout the pregnancy, and that she was just about two months pregnant. I could work with that. I didn't have a choice, and I had to be practical. I figured we had about six more months of Molly.

Six months turned into just a few weeks. Molly started to call in sick a few days after telling me about the surprise pregnancy. I had gone to work with morning sickness throughout my pregnancy with Rebecca. Why couldn't Molly? I would have thought that tough Molly could have worked through it. Maybe hers was way worse than mine had been? She said it was. I couldn't make her come to work, and so for the first time in what was then two and half years as a working mom, I had to miss work because I had no childcare. My boss was as understanding as she could be, having been a working mom herself, but I knew it was my responsibility to remedy the situation. In between working from home and taking care of Joey and Rebecca, I began the search for yet another nanny.

Health Reasons

We gave our fourth nanny, Julie, the week off in between Christmas and New Year's as Neil and I had both taken off work. We spent the week with the kids, doing little day trips and visiting out-of-town family that had come in for the winter break. It was a really nice week. That uninterrupted family time was great for all of us, but everyone was ready to get back into our regular routine come January. Joey loved his preschool even more as he got older and made more friends. Baby Rebecca grew to respond really well to nanny Julie, and Neil and I had lots to do back at our respective offices.

So on that first Monday after the holiday break, I was a bit concerned after nanny Julie was late for work. After thirty minutes, I called her cell phone and left a message. Another half hour passed. I called my office and apologetically explained that I'd be in late that day, even though I suspected I might not be in at all that day. Where the hell was Julie, and why wasn't she picking up her phone?

It was early afternoon when I got a call from her boyfriend, Nick. Julie was in the hospital, he explained. Apparently she had suffered from bulimia, among other eating disorders, for years, and she had taken a lot of diet pills over the holiday break. She was very sick. I literally had to lift my bottom lip up to meet my top lip so that I could speak. To say I was shocked was an understatement, although by that point you would have thought that nothing nanny-related could surprise me.

Nick stopped by our house later that afternoon to deliver nanny Julie's copy of our house keys back to us. In the meantime, while the kids napped I got on the horn. I called the nanny agency and my friend and nanny mentor, Stacey. Stacey gave me the name of the baby gym teacher who she had recently found out was looking for extra babysitting work. I was concerned about nanny Julie's health, but I needed to get back to work soon, especially after the long break. I was becoming a bit numb to all the nanny drama.

Nick and I exchanged pleasantries, and with a quick and very uncomfortable hug, I had my house keys back and my nanny taken away from me. Nanny Julie had only lasted seven months. I thought back to the interview with her and how she had brought up her weight loss issue with us. *Should I have read into that more?* I wondered. People do lose weight without being bulimic and taking diet pills. I wondered if she had thrown up in our bathroom while watching our kids or popped diet pills while driving them around. I really couldn't go there. The kids were safe and sound, and they needed a new nanny.

Rachel's Rules

GETTING DUMPED

There is no getting around it. Getting dumped is not fun. It's not fun for you, for your children, and in most cases, it's not fun for your nanny. It will feel like you've been abandoned—like you and your children are being left behind by someone that you loved and trusted. Try not to go there. Remind yourself that at the end of the day, your nanny is an employee, and has a life beyond taking care of your children. What were the odds that she would stay with you forever? Probably not so high, right? Remind yourself of this fact when you do get dumped, because eventually you will.

I was caught off-guard when most of our nannies left us, but in retrospect, I probably shouldn't have been. Each of our younger nannies was in a very transitory stage of her life, so she was bound to leave at some point. Although I never could have predicted the pregnancy and the bulimia, I should have at least considered the possibilities.

To avoid these kinds of situations, think long and hard about all potential possibilities and ask a lot of questions during the interview process. Do your homework. Examine how long each potential nanny worked for her last family, and consider if that candidate will be a life-long career nanny. That's about all you can do. Everything else is just a roll of the dice.

☙ 13 ☙

You're Fired

I've only had to fire one person in my professional life so far, and that was hard—really hard. The young man who worked for me as an assistant marketing manager at the magazine company in New York was very bright and seemed to be a hard worker when I first hired him. He also got along pretty well with the rest of our group, but that didn't last too long. After about six months on the job, I found that he wasn't getting his work done on time, and when he turned it in to me late, it had way too many mistakes. I ended up spending a lot of time cleaning up his messes. It got to the point where I couldn't get my work done because I was correcting his. I had a long talk about him with my boss, and we decided that we, actually I, would have to let him go.

I was so nervous to give him the news. As nicely as I could, I explained that it just wasn't working out on both ends. I gave him his two weeks' notice. He didn't take it so well, and I got to see his angry side. Not fun. He eventually cleaned out his office, and after two very long and awkward weeks, he finally left. I had to clean out his voicemail box after he was gone, and I got to listen to messages from his friends inquiring about his mean boss

. . . me. Those weren't fun to listen to. I knew, however, that I was doing the right thing—for me, my group, our company, and probably for him in the long-run.

Firing a nanny was even harder for me. It's not like firing a regular employee. It almost feels like firing a member of your family. You have to tell the person you've entrusted with taking care of your kids day after day that you feel that she is no longer fit to do so, and that she is no longer welcome in your house.

Had No Choice

Our fifth nanny, Alice, had been with us for nearly three years when I discovered things she was doing on that job that didn't sit well with me and with Neil. My friend Stacey's nanny Mariella dropped off Joey at our house one day after school, and it looked like no one was home. After ringing the front doorbell several times, nanny Alice came to the door. Mariella could tell that she had woken Alice up. Alice had pillow marks on her face, and she seemed a little out of it. Mariella reported the incident back to her boss Stacey, and then Stacey filled me in. It was an awkward conversation. I could tell that Stacey didn't want to have to narc out my nanny, but she also felt an obligation to tell me that my nanny was sleeping on the job. Mariella felt it was important too, and Mariella had gotten pretty close with Alice over the years. I appreciated everyone's honesty.

When I confronted nanny Alice on the matter, she assured me that Rebecca was asleep upstairs. She explained that she just needed a quick rest, and that she was always awake by the time Joey got home. *Always? So this napping on the job thing had become part of the routine?* I thought of George Costanza, finding the perfect spot under his desk to nap at work. That *Seinfeld* episode was so funny. This real life episode? Not so much. After a long talk with my friend Stacey, who was, after all, my original nanny-finding mentor, Stacey advised me to let Alice go. She felt that nanny Alice had exhibited unacceptable behavior. I didn't know what to do.

I knew it wasn't a great situation, but I couldn't pull the trigger. Alice had gone through treatment for her cancer several months prior to the napping bust. She was cancer free, which was great news, but I imagined that she was probably still very tired from her health crisis. I gave her a break. I did, at that point, clearly understand that nanny Alice didn't have the energy required to look after the kids in the way that we had originally expected. She probably never had. Perhaps my initial instinct about her being too old or too heavy to be our nanny was a good one? Or maybe things had changed over time as she had gotten too comfortable with us, and as the kids had gotten bigger? Maybe I had become too close to her, and I had made the lines blurred? I wasn't sure, but I knew that something would have to change.

All of our previous nannies had left on their own accord. I guess I had assumed that nanny Alice would one day leave us too. Although it was hard to have the nannies leave us, I was beginning to think that it might be harder to have to tell them to leave. I couldn't imagine doing it, especially to nanny Alice.

Neil thought nanny Alice had gotten too comfortable working for us long before I did, and not in the good kind of comfortable way. He felt that I let too many things slide with her, and that she took advantage of me a lot. Nanny Alice did have a pretty cushy set up. We paid her nicely—significantly more than we had ever paid any other nanny, partially because she had more experience, and also because that was her going rate. By that point we were paying her to have her own free time during the mornings when both kids were at school. There were only so many errands she could run for us. Yes, she was good with our kids, but that seemed to matter less and less. After a while, I finally came to understand that I was being taken advantage of. One final incident made my decision to fire nanny Alice a lot easier than I had ever imagined.

An acquaintance of mine, Blaire, approached me at a barbecue one Saturday afternoon and told me that she had run into nanny Alice out to lunch with a friend of hers one Wednesday afternoon. When Blaire asked nanny Alice where my kids were, she explained that Joey was in school and Rebecca was napping back at Alice's house while Alice's husband watched her in their crib. Blaire told me how she thought that was so cool of me to feel comfortable enough with Alice and her family and to have that kind of a set up. At least that's what she told me. She probably thought I was an idiot for allowing that to happen. At that moment, as my heart sank, I tried to keep a smile on my face, not wanting to let on that I had no idea what went on at my house while I was at work. I felt like a complete fool. I felt stupid for trusting nanny Alice so much. I felt guilty for leaving my daughter in the care of someone who left her to nap in a strange crib, and then I felt anger. I was really angry. There was a new boss in town—me.

I was just plain furious by the time we got home from the party. I couldn't let it sit even though Neil thought it might be best to wait until Monday morning to talk to nanny Alice about this in person. I knew myself, and I knew that I couldn't let it go the rest of the weekend. I called nanny Alice that night. When I asked her about the incident she casually apologized and said that she should have told me about it. I made it very clear to her that I was paying her to watch my kids at our house. Going out to lunch with a friend and leaving baby Rebecca at her house under the care of someone else, even if it was her husband, was completely unacceptable.

"I'm really sorry, Rach," she said. "I knew I should have said something to you after I ran into Blaire." *After she had run into Blaire? Was that the only red flag for her?* Alice knew she had been busted, but she had hoped that Blaire would not spill the beans. I was grateful that Blaire had. Even the casual tone in nanny Alice's voice had begun to bother me. I started to notice how she always called me "Rach." Only my good friends called me Rach. Nanny Alice was way too casual and comfortable with me. I knew that I was partially to blame for how comfortable nanny Alice had become around me, and then I blamed myself more for letting it get to that point.

I knew that I had made life too easy for all of our nannies. I had always wanted them to feel at ease working for me and for Neil. I wanted them to love our children as if they were their own. I also wanted them to like me. I figured that if they liked me, then they wouldn't let me down. Wrong again. I should have taken a page from Stacey's book and been firmer with my nannies, laying out many of the guidelines and house rules ahead of time. That could have prevented a lot of heartache and break-ups. It didn't matter so much then. I had to deal with the nanny Alice situation at hand.

"You can't always blame yourself," Neil said to me. "Alice was great for a while—she really was—but it's time to move on. You know that," he explained, right as usual. I knew it. I couldn't look back. I could only look forward. My dad always told me that.

I took about a week to think things through. After weighing lots of different options, I realized that come fall, and it was well into summer at that point, I could make our childcare situation work differently. Joey was about to start full-day kindergarten, and Rebecca could go to her preschool every day until 2:30 p.m. I could make it work by just having an after-school sitter three days a week. I felt I had the perfect excuse to let nanny Alice go.

Neil and Stacey repeatedly told me that I didn't need any excuse to let her go. I could just fire her. That was still tough for me. I took the easy, nonconfrontational way out of it. I laid out my new childcare set-up to nanny Alice and explained that we would no longer need her. I blamed my letting her go more on finances and logistics, and made it less about her poor job performance. Did it really matter at that point? Nanny Alice would soon be gone, and I didn't want to upset her while she was still taking care of my kids for the month of August. I also didn't want to burn any bridges. My father had given me that sound advice when I was much younger. He was so right about that.

Nanny Alice took the news pretty well. I really don't think that she suspected I was letting her go for any other reason than scheduling. Yes, nanny Alice knew that she had been busted on the job, but I think she thought that she could get away with it for as long as I needed her.

Stacey felt like she had no choice but to fire her second nanny Serena, but she was more up-front and honest about the whole thing. Serena had worked well, caring for Stacey's kids as they grew from a family with one little boy to a family with three little boys over the years. Nanny Serena seemed to have it all under control when the rules were simpler, but when things got more complicated, nanny Serena was no longer up for the job.

Stacey's youngest, Will, like my daughter Rebecca, was a late crawler. Stacey became concerned and took Will to see an occupational therapist to help him along. The therapist worked with baby Will on a weekly basis, and gave Stacey a list of exercises to do every day. The therapist also had a list of rules for the whole family to abide by in order to get Will moving. One of the rules was that he should not be in his car seat too much. Stacey clearly explained these rules to nanny Serena, explicitly telling her that she should only have Will in the car when she was picking up their oldest son at school. Baby Will should be taken out of the car seat when they got home, and he should be on the floor trying to move around at home.

Stacey had to remind nanny Serena about this rule several times when she came home to find baby Will sitting in the car seat on the floor while Serena dealt with the other kids. Stacey knew that it was tough to manage her household of three boys, and it was sometimes easier to leave the baby in the car seat. But easy wouldn't fly with Stacey. It was too important for Will's development.

Stacey drew the line when she came home from work one day and Serena told her that they spent all day at home so that Will could do his exercises. As nanny Serena gave her the report, Stacey found receipts out on the counter from all the places Serena had gone that day—with the children in the car. That was it. Stacey could not tolerate being lied to and having her son's motor development suffer as a result of her nanny's decisions. Stacey talked it over with her husband Phil that night, and then fired nanny Serena the next morning when she came to work.

And on that morning that Stacey fired Serena, Serena showed up on my doorstep in tears. Stacey gave her two weeks' notice, and although nanny Serena was caught off-guard, and also terribly upset, she still had to care for the kids. That morning caring for the kids meant getting them off to school and picking up Joey on the way, as it was her turn to drive the carpool.

I was surprised to see Serena in tears as I put Joey's large backpack on his very small back and tried to move along the morning so that I could get to work. Serena let it all out.

"Stacey fired me," she said in between her sniffles. "I don't know what I did wrong. I tried really hard, and I love those kids," she explained to me.

"I know you tried hard," I said. "And I know how much you love the boys. They love you too and so does Stacey. It was just time for a change," I managed to get out.

I felt bad for Serena, but I didn't want to get into it with her. I knew that Stacey had not been happy with nanny Serena for a while, but I could have used a little heads-up on what went down at their house that morning before Serena showed up at my house as a complete wreck. I was also a little concerned about Serena's state of mind that morning, and wondered if she should be driving the kids to school.

"Do you want me to drive the kids to school?" I calmly asked. "I really don't mind."

"No, no I'm fine," said Serena as she slowly got herself together. Once I saw that she had calmed down, I gave her a big and very awkward hug and then sent her on her way. That was the last I would see of nanny Serena.

I wasn't the one who fired her, but for some reason, that morning it felt like I was.

Easier to Lie

I sort of told a little white lie when I let nanny Alice go. I could have told her the truth. I could have explained to her that I was very upset at some of the things that she had done or not done while caring for my kids, but for me it was easier to lie—just a little bit. My mother used to say that there is nothing wrong with telling a little white lie every once in a while, especially if it would spare someone's feelings. I went with that. So did my college friend Alison, the New York City mom and advertising executive.

Alison's first nanny Gail appeared to be very good with her baby daughter Isabel. Every Monday morning, nanny Gail and Isabel went off to their baby music class. Alison always got great reports from Gail about how much little Isabel enjoyed the class. Nanny Gail often sang songs from the class with baby Isabel back at home.

One Monday afternoon, Alison received an unusual call at her office. It was from the baby music teacher.

"Alison, I teach your daughter's music class," said the woman on the other end of the phone. "Isabel is fine, but I wanted to let you know that today during class, her nanny left her in the circle of children and took a nap on the bleachers in the back of the room."

"Well, thanks for telling me. I really appreciate it," replied Alison. And with that, she hung up the phone.

Before she picked up the phone again to report back on the day's event to her husband, Nathan, Alison knew that she was going to fire nanny Gail. In Alison's book, leaving a baby in the middle of music class to go take a nap was definitely grounds for getting fired. I should have known this back when I had the opportunity to fire nanny Alice for sleeping on the job at my house. But Alison was a much quicker and better decision maker than I was. That was one of the qualities that I had always admired in her. Back in college, when we shared a house with six other girls, and I couldn't figure out which class to take or what sweater to wear, Alison chimed in with her opinion from across the hall, and the decision was made.

Nathan agreed with Alison's instinct. She would let nanny Gail go that evening. It was a done deal, and Alison soon figured out how she would fire her—she would lie. Alison subscribed to my mother's belief that it's sometimes just fine to tell a little white lie. Alison didn't want to deal with the conflict. She didn't want to get into it with nanny Gail. On Alison's subway ride and then walk home from work, she figured out a plan.

"I'm really sorry Gail," Alison explained as nanny Gail was cleaning up baby Isabel's dinner and preparing her for bath time, "but I have to let you go. I was laid off at work today, and since I won't be working for a while, I won't need a nanny anymore."

That was it. It was easy for Alison to tell the lie and avoid a messy confrontation. During nanny Gail's two week notice period, Alison networked like crazy and was able to find nanny Joan, who she employed until she and her family left the city years later.

The Gail incident was not completely behind them as Alison had imagined it would be. About six months after Alison had let nanny Gail go, Gail ran into baby Isabel and her new nanny Joan at the neighborhood playground. Gail had gotten a new job as a nanny for another family nearby, and recognized baby Isabel at the playground when accompanying the new children she was caring for. Nanny Joan didn't know why nanny Gail had been fired, but she did explain that she was the new nanny for Isabel. When nanny Joan reported back on the playground run-in to her boss, Alison was slightly embarrassed that she had been caught in the lie, but she let it go. She was good like that.

Growing Pains

There are instances when the firing is mutual and also amicable. Often this happens when the family outgrows the nanny, and the nanny also outgrows the family. This was the case for our third nanny, Molly, and the family that she worked for before coming to us. She took care of those kids for several years until they were old enough to take care of themselves after school. Nanny Molly was still in close touch with that family when she worked for us.

Sometimes there is a logistics issue that ends the relationship. When my friend Nina the lawyer and her family moved out to the suburbs from the city, they thought that they would no longer employ their nanny Liza. She had been with them for six years, and they were sad to see her go. Nanny Liza didn't want to leave them either. She figured out a way to make it work and make the hour-long drive out to the burbs to watch Nina's kids after school. This arrangement lasted for a year, but it started not to make sense to anyone.

Nanny Liza needed more hours, and Nina started to need less hours as her kids were in school for longer days. The commute added up in time and expenses for nanny Liza, and so she parted professional ways very amicably with Nina and her family. It's been over two years since nanny Liza stopped working for Nina, but they still see each other. Liza sometimes has Nina's children sleep over at her house. They had a great breakup, by anyone's standards.

Rachel's Rules

YOU'RE FIRED

It's never fun to fire someone, and I can imagine that it's really not fun to get fired. Try not to think about it so much. If you have to fire a nanny for whatever reason, then go ahead and do it. If you think you can't do it because you don't want to hurt anyone's feelings, then do what Alison and I did—just lie. What's the worst thing that can happen? Your lie will get uncovered one day on the swingset at an Upper West Side playground? It's too late by that point. You will have moved on.

Over the years, I learned that if and when you start to think that you should fire a nanny, you probably should have—a long time ago. Maybe I could have avoided getting dumped by so many of my nannies if I had taken the initiative and fired them first when things didn't feel right. You know, like when my baby son fell off the kitchen counter while in the care of our nanny Amy who was emptying the dishwasher, or when nanny Molly was out back behind our house smoking while Joey napped upstairs. I guess hindsight's 20/20, but I still do think about these things from time to time. If you are really lucky like my friend Nina, you won't really have to fire your nanny. You can fire each other for good and very understandable reasons.

≈ 14 ≈

Where Are They Now?

My mother used to say that I collected friends and I never let them go. She was kind of right. Since childhood, I've never lost a friend, only gained more. Neil makes fun of me for this as he tells me that I need to start letting people go.

"How can you keep up with so many people?" Neil sometimes asks me when I recount a story of a little reunion of sorts with friends from childhood, college, graduate school, or former places of work. I don't really know. It's just kind of in my blood. I feel lucky that I've come into contact with so many great people throughout the course of my life, and I don't want to let these people go. Why should I?

Not surprisingly, then, I still keep up with many of our former nannies. They seem to turn up in my life sometimes when I least expect it.

Baby Nurse Jackie

Baby nurse Jackie came back to our house to help out with Rebecca right after she was born. It went so well the second time around that I asked her to stay for a whole month. I also needed more help, as I had a C-section with Rebecca, and I was chasing after then-toddler Joey. Since that time, I've referred Jackie to so many friends and colleagues that my dad thinks I should get some kind of referral commission.

Nurse Jackie also worked for my friends Ellen, Jane, and Alison, plus my cousin, and several other friends, friends of friends, and relatives of friends. Jackie's list of clients looks a bit like a long and extended family tree, mixed in with a Venn diagram of people that I know. When Jackie couldn't work for one of my friends because she was already on another job, she sent other nurses from her group. Jackie's nursing friends worked for Suzanne, Leigh, and both of my sisters-in-law. One of my favorite pictures that sits on my bureau is of baby nurse Jackie, Alison, Jane, Leigh, me, and all of our children who Jackie directly or indirectly helped to care for. It reminds me how much Jackie helped all of us out when we needed her most.

Whenever Jackie worked for a friend or family member of mine, I tried to bring my kids to see her and visit on the job. This wasn't always possible, as she traveled as far as Florida, Nevada, and California to help out some of my friends. Nurse Jackie always commented about how big my kids were getting, and she usually said something nice about their behavior or their dispositions. I appreciated the sentiment, and always told her that had it not been for her, my kids probably would never have slept through the night. She laughed and responded with her signature, "No problem," and bright, toothy smile.

Jackie checks in with all of us through Facebook, emails, texts, and calls. She even stopped by my friend Jane's apartment recently while working for a family in Jane's neighborhood. Jackie also paid a visit to Alison one day to deliver a favorite dish to Alison's husband—roasted goat!

We've also gladly acted as references for Jackie over the years. Every few months I get a call from an expecting mother from somewhere in the country who is considering hiring Jackie as her baby nurse, and she wants my opinion. I always give Jackie a glowing reference. She had her quirks, of course, that we discovered when we lived with her, but she was so great. Those first few weeks of new parenthood would have been much tougher without her.

My favorite run-in with nurse Jackie happened last year in Philadelphia. I was at a 76ers basketball game at the Wells Fargo Center with Joey, then ten years old, a few of his friends, and some other moms. As Joey passionately cheered for his favorite NBA team and I ate popcorn while chatting with the moms, strangers in the stadium started to point to us and cheer too. Joey and I were on the Jumbotron! He was so excited. We waved and cheered too. Our fifteen minutes, well actually more like fifteen seconds, of fame were over.

Then my cell phone started going a little nuts as people watching the game at home had seen us on the screen. One person actually saw the Jumbotron in person because she was at the game. It was baby nurse Jackie. She texted me her seat number. Joey and I paid her a visit.

"What are you doing in Philly?" I asked. "And at a Sixers game?"

"Oh I love basketball! I'm taking care of a tiny baby here in Philly and the dad took me to the game," Jackie explained.

She introduced me to the dad, who I could tell was as enamored with Jackie as I had been when she first starting working for us.

"Where's the mom?" I asked, letting my curiosity get the best of me.

"She's home with the baby," said Jackie as she and the dad smiled at me and Joey too.

I got it, although I did recognize the absurdity of the situation. This family was paying nurse Jackie to care for their new baby and help out the mother. During that time, they took her out to a professional basketball game and left the mother at home to care for the baby. Nurse Jackie was an invaluable person to the family at the time, she loved basketball, and they wanted to keep her happy. That's just what you do, at least for baby nurse Jackie.

Nanny Molly

We kept in close contact with nanny Molly after she left us to have her baby. Even though I felt slighted that she left us so abruptly, I was still concerned for her wellbeing, and wanted to make sure she was feeling okay. So I checked in with her from time to time throughout her pregnancy. Her middle-of-the-night text woke me with news of the birth of her daughter, Monica. Monica was a happy and healthy baby, and Molly was going to stay home with her as long as she could make it work. When Monica was little, I would sometimes bring Joey and baby Rebecca over to Molly's house to visit. Monica was just a year younger than Rebecca, and the two little girls played nicely together.

As the years went on, we didn't keep in touch as closely as we used to, but I never deleted her contact information from my phone. I'm glad I didn't. Last summer when my father was going through a minor health crisis, his longtime housekeeper, who also worked for us, quit with no notice. I remembered that Molly had once cleaned houses professionally, so I called her up to see if she might be interested in working for my dad and for us.

It was great to catch up with Molly. Little Monica was already six years old and about to start first grade. Molly had opened up a flower shop of her own, and it was going really well. I had no idea that she had an interest in flowers. That was nanny Alice's specialty. Molly was not available to clean houses, but her cousin Tara was looking for work. My father hired her, I did too, and so did my brother. She is the best housekeeper we have ever had. Our house looks even better than it did when nanny Molly worked for us. And she is great at folding fitted sheets.

Nanny Alice

I needed a break from nanny Alice after she stopped working for us. I needed a break from the drama and the feeling that I was getting taken advantage of, but I don't think nanny Alice saw it that way. She kept up with me through Facebook—a lot. At that point, my writing career started to take off, and Alice always commented on my published articles after she read them. I appreciated her being my cheerleader, but I needed time. It was kind of a bad breakup, as far as I was concerned.

About a year after Alice was gone, I did see her again as she and her husband filled in at the very last minute to watch Joey and Rebecca one Saturday night when our college sitter canceled about an hour before she was supposed to show up. I debated calling nanny Alice, but I was sort of desperate and enough time had passed. It was good to see Alice and her husband again. The kids loved seeing her. I was glad we asked her, but that was the last time that we saw her.

I have run into some of her family members over the years, and I always make sure to tell them to send my best to nanny Alice. Like my father always said, never burn bridges.

Nanny Mariella

Nanny Mariella is still in my friend Stacey's life. Although Mariella now has two little kids of her own, she sometimes helps out Stacey with her boys when she is really in a bind. Mariella has watched Stacey's kids, now thirteen, ten, and eight, on those school vacation days when Stacey still has to work but the kids are at home. Mariella just brings her own kids with her to the house, and all of the boys have fun playing together.

Stacey has also hired Mariella to help out at parties in her home. I've done the same. I always enjoy seeing her and catching up. Mariella seems to get a kick out of seeing Joey and Rebecca now more grown up after all she did drive them to school in carpool for many years.

Nanny Mariella came to the rescue one night for my childhood friend Ellen, the human resources consultant. Ellen and Rob had never left their babies with anyone besides the grandparents for a Saturday night date night. There was one Saturday night when both sets of grandparents were away and they needed a sitter to attend a party—actually my fortieth birthday party. Ellen had interviewed a local college girl and hired her for the night. The girl called her just a few hours before the party to cancel on Ellen because there was a death in the family.

Ellen called me in a panic. She felt badly for the new sitter, but she really wanted to find someone so they could come to the party. I was touched that she was trying so hard to make it to the party.

"Rach," said Ellen. "I've been with you for just about every birthday since we were little kids. "I'm not missing the fortieth," she very sweetly told me.

In the midst of shoveling my driveway to get ready for the party during a January snowstorm, I sent a text to Stacey asking if Mariella might want to babysit for Ellen, even on such short notice. Stacey thought it was worth a try. So I sent a group text to nanny Mariella (completely out of the blue) and to Ellen explaining the situation. Sure enough, Mariella was able to make it work. She is now Ellen and Rob's regular Saturday night sitter.

Nanny Liza

Nanny Liza became a grandmother-type figure to Nina's children over the course of the seven years that she took care of them. Nanny Liza still keeps in close touch with Nina, Mark, and the kids. When Nina and Mark need someone to watch the kids for the weekend, they call nanny Liza. She is always more than happy to help out. Not surprisingly to Nina, nanny Liza makes it a fun weekend full of adventure for the kids.

Nanny Rori

While Suzanne's nanny Rori moved on to a new career in catering, she still watches Suzanne's kids from time to time. Suzanne likes to keep up with Rori and really does take pride in seeing how nicely her young nanny has grown up. She's almost like a third child to Suzanne, albeit one who had the job of caring for her two other children for several years.

When the holidays roll around, Rori still takes Nina's son Ryan to see Santa Claus, and she still hangs his stocking up in her house. And the instructions on how to work the toaster oven still hang in Suzanne's kitchen in homage to nanny Rori.

Not Sure Where They Are Now

We never heard from our first nanny, Amy, after that fateful phone call the morning that we left for our family beach vacation. I think of her when I see a Penn State sticker on a car, or when I empty the dishwasher, and when I kiss now eleven-year-old Joey goodnight on his smooth forehead—no trace of the bump in sight.

Nanny Ellie has never reached out to us since she left us for the teaching job. And I didn't feel like I had to keep up with her, especially since she asked me for more money on her last day to pay her sister. I explained that I would pay her sister directly. I sometimes wonder if and where she is teaching now. Perhaps my kids will one day end up in her classroom?

I wonder about nanny Julie too. I hope she was able to beat her battle with bulimia. A few years after she left us, I covered a story on eating disorders for a Philadelphia newspaper. I interviewed many young women suffering from anorexia and bulimia and spoke to a few experts in the field. I learned how many bulimics covered up their illness so well and for so long. That was nanny Julie. I really can't imagine what she was going through, and all the while she was taking care of my kids.

Rachel's Rules

WHERE ARE THEY NOW?

You never know when you are going to run into a former nanny. Perhaps you will be on the Jumbotron one day at a professional sporting event and your former nanny or baby nurse will be there too? More likely you will need your nanny to help out with your kids down the road. As a working mom, you always need a list of backup sitters. Former nannies know your kids just about as well as you do, and they are great resources to help you out in a pinch. My phone contains the numbers of too many former nannies and sitters to count.

So try as best as you can never to burn bridges. There are times, of course, when this is simply not possible. If the breakup was really bad, I get it. It's time to make that clear break and move on. Delete the number. But try, if you can, to make the breakup as amicable as possible. Take the high road, be the bigger person, do what you have to do. As the old saying goes, you can kill more flies with honey than with vinegar. Remember that. Even if it sounds really hard, try it. You'll be glad you did one day, trust me. You may even one day rehire a former nanny. Sonny rehired her first nanny Colleen, the hugging nanny, as her fourth nanny.

Epilogue

It's been over a decade since baby nurse Jackie walked in through our kitchen door, and nearly just as long since we hired Amy to be our first nanny. In that time, we've had four more nannies come in and out of our lives, in addition to two after-school college sitters.

My kids no longer need all-day care because of their school schedules. My career also took an unexpected turn. Shortly after I let nanny Alice go, I left my job in marketing to become a full-time writer. My mother's long battle with cancer prompted me to write a book about our relationship and her valiant effort in fighting the disease. After the book came out, I was offered freelance assignments for various papers, magazines, and blogs. Then another book followed.

I feel lucky—very lucky. I am now able to work around my childrens' schedules and no longer require a nanny. I do still struggle to find a sitter at the last minute when I have a story to cover or a deadline that has crept up on me, but I make it work.

My kids seem to be growing and thriving, and, most importantly to me, they are happy kids. They managed not to get scarred by the revolving door of nannies in their younger years, the bump on the head, the being left in a crib in a strange house, the smoking nanny, and more.

I am grateful that I was able to find and hold on to our nannies for as long as I could, even though the situations weren't always ideal. I had to kiss a lot of frogs, and still I'm not sure I ever found my prince. I'm not even sure one really exists. I am grateful that I was able to find and employ, for the most part, good people to care for my kids so that I could hold on to a piece of myself that was very important to me—my career.

Here's a little secret. There is no such thing as a perfect nanny. Mary Poppins is a fictional character. Even nanny Louise, who long ago worked for my boss Jennifer in New York, had her own flaws, or so Jennifer later told me. Unless we working moms can figure out a way to clone ourselves, and I don't see that happening anytime soon, we will continue to have our own nanny struggles. It's just another part of the job description for a working mom.

If you take anything away from my stories and the stories of my friends, I hope you will remember to give yourself a break every now and then. Take it one day at a time, always communicate with your nanny, have a sense of humor, have fun with your kids, and take a deep breath. You can do it. I know you can.

Acknowledgments

This is the book that I said I would write, and my friends said I had to write it. They were, and continue to be, my biggest cheerleaders. I am eternally grateful for their encouragement, their time, their reads, and their feedback. To the growing-up friends, the college friends, the grad school friends, and the mom friends, thank you for sharing with me the details of your children, your nannies, your careers, and your lives. Thank you for telling me that I had something here, even when I wasn't sure that I did. Thank you to my father, who read every word and laughed out loud along the way, as only he could with his eternal optimistic attitude that I wish I could bottle. To my sweet brother, who asked almost too many questions, but probably just enough to make sure I would get it right. Thank you to Aunt Linda, my unofficial editor, and Aunt Jo, my unofficial publicist. Thank you to ASJA participants for encouraging me to put my nanny stories together and for suggesting a framework for how I might do this. Thank you to the wonderful and understanding editorial team at Turning Stone. Thanks to the great people at Starbucks on State Street in Newtown, PA for letting me camp out and write day after day, and for making my soy chai tea latte extra hot. Thank you to my employers who understood when I had to leave work early because of a nanny emergency. Thank you to the nannies I employed over the years. Although we didn't always get it down perfectly, we did manage to work together to raise some pretty great kids. And to those kids, Joey and Rebecca, thank you for being you—fun, inquisitive, creative, and loving kids. Thanks for putting up with the revolving door of nannies in our house (like you had a choice!). Thanks for all the snuggles and for understanding when I had my head in my laptop. Lastly, for Neil—that great guy, the salt of the earth who's got it all going on—always. Thank you for your constant support and unconditional everything. I couldn't have done any of this without you, and why would I want to? It's just that much more fun with you.

About the Author

Rachel Levy Lesser is a regular featured blogger on *The Huffington Post*. Her work has appeared in *The Philadelphia Jewish Exponent*, *PHL Metropolis*, *AND Magazine*, *The Glamour Magazine Blog* and *Bucks Local News*. Rachel is the author of the memoir *Shopping for Love* and the children's book *My Name is Rebecca Romm Named After My Mother's Mom*. Her essay on mother loss was published in *Letters From Motherless Daughters*. Rachel received her BA summa cum laude from the University of Pennsylvania and her MBA from the Ross School of Business at the University of Michigan. She lives in Newtown, Pennsylvania with her husband and two children and currently no nanny.

www.ingramcontent.com/pod-product-compliance
Lightning Source LLC
Chambersburg PA
CBHW022019090426
42739CB00006BA/204